I AM YOUR
SIGN

THE SECRET TO
UNLEASHING REVIVAL
AND IGNITING A
NATIONAL AWAKENING

SEAN SMITH

DESTINY IMAGE® PUBLISHERS, INC.
P.O. Box 310, Shippensburg, PA 17257-0310

"Promoting Inspired Lives"

This book and all other Destiny Image, Revival Press, MercyPlace, Fresh Bread, Destiny Image Fiction, and Treasure House books are available at Christian bookstores and distributors worldwide.

For a U.S. bookstore nearest you, call 1-800-722-6774.
For more information on foreign distributors, call 717-532-3040.
Reach us on the Internet: www.destinyimage.com.

ISBN 13 TP: 978-0-7684-3976-2
ISBN 13 Ebook: 978-0-7684-8932-3

For Worldwide Distribution, Printed in the U.S.A.
1 2 3 4 5 6 7 8 9 10 11 / 13 12 11

Dedication

I dedicate this book to my wife Barbara, who has been such a huge source of inspiration and allowed me the space to spend crazy hours preparing this life work for publication. She has served our family in a way that has demonstrated Jesus tangibly. She has prayed for and encouraged me every step of the way. Without her I would not be who I am, nor would I have been in position to be a voice for a spiritual revolution. She is an example of a Woman of God who has gone for it in the Kingdom in every way she possibly could, and yet has left her mark on Brandon, Brittany, and me in ways that we are forever grateful. I love you, Babe.

Acknowledgments

There are many special people who have blessed my life and invested in the development of the work that I have benefitted from greatly. These individuals have helped me be in position to take on and finish such a challenging undertaking.

Brandon—I am steadily amazed as I see God unfold His greatness in your life. You have lived a set-apart lifestyle that is a SIGN to your generation. Our talks have gone from my challenging you, to a mutual sharpening as you have matured in your anointing and character. You have such a high call, don't settle!

Brittany—You have been and always will be my Princess. You have made me so sanctified proud as you have kept your convictions and grown in your giftings. You have inspired me as I have seen the strength of your faith and the way you seek to encourage your friends. The world is truly the limit for you, shoot for God's highest!

Nina Walls—Thanks Mom, you have modeled hard work and love through the sacrifices you've made. You have never given up, no matter how tough things got, and that has rubbed off on me. Thanks, I love you!

Anthony—Hey Bro, thanks for all that you do. Your gifting and calling never cease to amaze me as you figure out how to make things better. I appreciate your servant's heart and looking out for a brotha!

Frank and Kendra—You have supported us in so many ways over the last 20-plus years. You guys have always believed in us and have been there for us in more ways than we could ever count. Your encouragement has gotten us through. Love you guys!

Marissa (Missy)—You have been such a breath of fresh air and SSM/PBI first intern, not to mention an awesome niece. Thanks for your major help on this project and correspondence. We love ya!

Banning—You are my brotha in so many ways. Thanks for your advice and Barnabas-like endorsement and encouragement. Running with Jesus Culture has been such a blast!

Pastor Sam and Linda—You guys have always looked out for my family and challenged me to be the best I can be, while rooting us on. Much love and gratitude.

Gaylord and Patti—You guys have been Dad and Mom to us. Thanks for looking out for our souls and life investment over the years. We love you guys!

Mario and Mechelle—Thanks so much for believing in us and giving us our first office space when we began as evangelists. Your encouragement has definitely propelled us to further heights. We love you both!

Dee Davis—Your selfless intercession has been such a blessing to not only this project, but also to our fam. Thanks so much and the Smiths love you!

Jesus—Most of all, I am indebted and eternally grateful to *You,* my majestic King and Deliverer. I thank You for putting the call of God on my broken life. You rescued me so I could help rescue others!

Revival

Written by Jonno Rossol
Twitter: @jonnorossol

A word often found, oft thought understood.
A word to prompt souls to take hold of what's good.
Three syllables brought,
And through linguistics wrought,
Into a loaded term of which we always seem to fall short:

Revival.

So what does it mean? Cause most of our biblical examples
Are really obscenely graphic when revival arrives.
As a raw generation thrashes and strives
To tear the thin veil and make Heaven arrive
In the great and the smalls of their everyday lives.

Usually ignited by one Pioneer
Or two or three who hate religion and fear.
Does it come wrapped up in a neat parcel size?
No, it comes to free sinners and confounds the wise.
But in our image of Church we buy hype and lies,
And convince one another that
We must sterilize the way we do God.
And keep Him locked in a box.
Yet no matter how well we make them,
He still picks the locks
On the constraints we put up
And in the dark where we hide
Because His love is so radical He cannot abide
By watching His people be tricked and then lied to
About their destiny to be His glorious Bride

So He raises up warriors, gems in the rough.
Those who see affliction, and then say enough.
To the disinformation of the prince of the air.
Those who see through his guise to what's really there:

A powerless prowler who tried to conquer the One
Who was created, but was still there before time had begun.

You see, the devil said, "I will," in the Book of Isaiah.
But Adam learned the hard way that he's the principal liar
Offering fruits and life and a way to climb higher.
Like "You want greatness? Psych, now burn in the fire"
And we buy this lie with credit we don't own,
And the debt piles up so you can't pay on your own.
So we work even harder 'til we're catching our breath
But it's all just as futile 'cause those wages are death
And it takes something more than human power can boast,
Because even the greatest man will only be almost.
So when we're cornered and lost and just want death to arrive

When we're coding on the table and the crash cart's alive
His spiritual defibrillator dials up to high
Love looks us in the eyes and says "I've come to revive."

Come! We must get past our notion of "clean"
Since when was the surgeon's table ever pristine?
God is the surgeon who scrapes from the heart
All the scars and the cuts 'til we're all set apart
Yes it is messy, and yes there's a cost
But trading your pride to redeem all the lost
Is a mate's rate like you would never believe
So cash in your pride lest the Holy Spirit grieve
Over missed chances to bring home a son or a daughter
Because His vessel wasn't ready to contain Holy water
It often seems more than our emotions can bear
But God needs more than emotion when receiving His heir

Christ was born in the midst of a mess
It doesn't offend Him, which places even more stress
On the truth that revival is not small and neat
It's God's presence invading and purging like heat
The iniquities of my broken body, clean in a heartbeat
And nothing remains but the name that's so sweet:

Jesus

The one who was sent down and came
Died on the cross not in vain
Who before our foundation was ever lain
Was found to be perfect but still bound and slain
Is waiting in Heaven for the Bride's full arrival
One question remains: Are you living revival?

Contents

Foreword by Mike Bickle 15

Foreword by Winkie Pratney 17

Not Your Ordinary Introduction 19

1. Jonah Speaks Sign Language 25

2. Make Way For *Metanoia* 43

3. Tipping Points and the
   Third Person of the Trinity 59

4. Pulling the Rip Cord
   of a Modern-Day Revival 77

5. The Combination Code
   of a Divine Moment 95

6. Moved Upon to
   Embody a Movement 109

7. Forging a Revival Culture 125

8.   Twenty Minutes to a Revival:
     Spontaneity and a Spiritual Awakening. 143

9.   Becoming a Mouthpiece
     of an Awakening 155

10. Mainstreaming the Miraculous:
     Now *This* I've Got to See!. 171

11. End-Time Ingatherings
     and the Harvest of Revival 187

12. Chosen to Change
     the Course of History 203

     Endnotes 227

Foreword by Mike Bickle

For years, I have deliberately followed the early revivalists such as Jonathan Edwards, David Brainerd, Count Zinzendorf, and some of the Puritan writers; and have taken on their theology of an unprecedented ingathering of souls at the end off the age.

I'm convinced that the fullness of Joel 2 is yet to be seen and it will have a worldwide scope to it, where all flesh who love Jesus will have dreams and see visions. This will be the greatest and fullest manifestation of the Kingdom of God, which will culminate in an unprecedented revival in which believers will experience everything that Joel prophesied. There will be an empowered witness of the gospel that will trigger a phenomenal harvest of souls.

In 1982, in a dirty little motel room in Cairo, Egypt, the Lord spoke to me about an end-time outpouring of the Spirit. I trembled and wept as the Spirit spoke to me in a way that I've never know before or since. The Spirit said, "I will change the understanding and expression of Christianity on earth in one generation". I understood that this revival would be His sovereign initiative and that God Himself was going to make this drastic change in Christianity across the earth. The Father will change the understanding of Christianity and the way unbelievers view the Church. They will witness God's glorious yet terrifying power through God's people. God will change the way the Church expresses His life, with power demonstrations backed by holy love.

I have known Sean for about twenty years and believe that the Father has prepared him to carry a definite prophetic message. He is a man with and unusual passion for Jesus and the Kingdom of God. I have seen his life and ministry up close and really believe in him. Sean is a needed voice to this generation. I love his message of revival and his evangelistic heart that burns for the harvest.

His book, *I Am Your Sign* is a timely God appointed summons to the Bride of Christ to position herself for the massive harvest that Joel prophesied and the Puritans believed for. Sean's book combines both the rich history of revivals and the prophetic edge which is sure to call forth from the reader a burning heart to witness what the Father has in His heart for the end times. As we have seen in our *Onething* conferences and at IHOPU, there is a hunger in this generation that has been divinely placed which points towards escalation of the Spirit's activity. There is a coming great visitation of God and *I Am Your Sign* will encourage, equip and inspire you to be right in the midst of what the Father has up His sleeves and in His heart for this hour. I believe in Sean and this book, and I highly recommend this work to your list of must reads.

Mike Bickle is the director of the International House of Prayer of Kansas City or IHOP-KC (www.IHOP.org). He is the author of several books including Passion for Jesus, Growing in the Prophetic, The Pleasures of Loving God, After God's Heart, and Prayers to Strengthen Your Inner Man.

Foreword by Winkie Pratney

Every now and then you run slam-dunk into a fresh vision of God's greatness, something unveiled somehow by someone from somewhere off the beaten path pursued by so many.

It is a special joy to meet such a seeker; one who has paid a quiet price and done the sacred time to see God's work for themselves with new eyes and a burning heart. History is rife with those who have faced the darkness of the soul and in their quest have come face to face with the only One who still carries a spot-lit future for our lost world.

Revival is a distinct watch-word, at once so desired and yet so often mistaken or misunderstood that some have simply given up the search as something almost harmless if not currently hopeless. A girl recently said to me, "I have never seen a revival. I have come to believe that thought it may have been true once, it is now no longer possible."

I was saddened but sympathetic; that one young life should live so long with both godly parents and a divine calling and yet not see His work affect our world. Revival is not our goal lest we make it another form of idolatry; it is always a description of His divine operation, not some mere ambition for adjustment. It has been my privilege to see such visits as well as multitudes of records from generation after generation of precious saints who not only sought His face for restored presence, but really experienced it in their own time. We do so need again that real encounter from heaven, not made by human hands.

I Am Your Sign is a care-filled composite of Scripture, supernatural history and personal story bringing together some of the great Bible themes clothed with cutting-edge analysis in current contexts. Sean's great book is not only filled with vision, but a good read from a hungry heart may very well bring you face to face with a visitation.

WINKIE PRATNEY
South Auckland, New Zealand

Not Your Ordinary Introduction

Never let a generation grow up without that knowledge of Divine things which may contain the germ of national revival in years to come.—Rhys Bevan Jones

The Genesis of a Revivalist

There are some things you just can't ease into. Some things, by their very nature, don't have a welcome mat, user-friendly tutorial, or on-ramp access. Swimming was one of those things for me. I learned to swim when I was seven at my cousin's house in Hayward, California. My uncle simply threw me in the deep end of their pool. I sank before I quickly learned to doggie-paddle enough to make it to the surface. Writing about revival and the making of revivalists is an assignment that calls people to cannonball into the daunting, deep end of the pool. There's nothing undemanding or unchallenging about unleashing a holy takeover of a hostile world in the name of Jesus. Yet, our heavenly Father is in the business of helping people turn intimidating waters into paths of destiny. Consider the Red Sea crossing.

I Am Your Sign is about becoming an epicenter of awakening in your world. A watershed outpouring is about to be released on your world. This book is written to ignite you for a mighty wave of God activity that is about to sweep into this generation. With that, I want you to open your heart and join me on an epic journey of discovery and transformation. This rite of passage has historic implications that might save a nation or two. In *Cataracts of Revival*, G.J. Morgan says:

> God is always preparing His workers in advance; and when the hour is ripe He brings them upon stage; and men look and wonder upon a career of startling triumph which God had been preparing for a lifetime. God is preparing His revivalists still, so when the opportunity comes He can fit them into their places in a moment while the world wonders where they came from.[1]

In many regions, there is an organic, grassroots movement that is sensing a major outpouring of the Spirit is ready to drop. Fresh and exceptional things are about to take place through God's people around the world. In this season, God is calling forth underground revivalists to emerge from the crowd and take the stage for a moral revolution. I'm convinced that an epic spiritual awakening is rumbling and the revival of all revivals is coming—but a people must be made ready.

God wrote the script of your life before the doctor had the chance to slap your glutes (see Ps. 139:15-16). Yet, the script of your life isn't going to happen automatically without you consenting and contending for it. You and I are responsible to discover that all-important script. Part of the script can be found deep within your heart. The other part? It is in the Father's counsel, awaiting your pursuit.

Youth of today feel like they're inheriting a world the night after a long, bad party, where all that's left is trying to clean up and find leftovers. Not only is our planet threatened by ecological crises, wars, and an economy on life support, but we also have a society where a sense of purpose has been sucked right out of people.

Our world has many problems and one solution—the radical spiritual surgery of God on a society: in short, revival. Revival is the ultimate spiritual resuscitation. Mary Stewart Relfe says, "A revival is...a sudden demonstration of God's irresistible power. Nation-shaking and history making, this mighty righteous revolution transforms the character of a nation practically overnight."[2] Some, however, think that the United States is beyond repair or that it's too late to see redemptive purposes released in this generation.

Imagine a wrestler inches from having his second shoulder pinned down, ending the match in defeat. All the onlookers are envisioning the inevitable conclusion. Yet, the seemingly defeated wrestler, in one move, flips the dominant wrestler on top, making him a defeated victim on the bottom. That surprising, peculiar move is the spiritual equivalent of a revival. Just when it looks like God's people are down for the count, Heaven unleashes the "reversal move" of the ages.

God's gift to a nation is a generation of emerging revivalists who have both: 1) the prophetic sense of what the Father wants to release, and 2) the anointing of the supernatural combined with a tenacious love of an evangelist to stand out. These "signs from Heaven" in human form serve as a firewall against moral decay.

I've had a stirring in my heart for revival that has gone to new levels in a recent season but began years ago. Recently, I found one of my early Bibles, and written in it was the phrase, "Revival would be the fulfillment of my dreams." I guess you could say God put revival in my spiritual DNA early on. I got called to ministry through a series of visions of coliseums full of a massive harvest combined with miracles.

God wants to change the things you have been defined by. Our current brand of Christianity has struggled to some point, because we have not been saturated with God's presence and become carriers of it. Selwyn Hughes says, "The level of spiritual energy in the contemporary Christian church seems no match for the fast-developing agnosticism of this postmodern generation."[3] We need revival so that we don't fall behind in the race for hearts in the upcoming generation. The steel punch (a term used to describe when God breaks open the heavens over a people) of God has happened before, and it can occur again. Our coming revision of this revival dynamic will be mightier and will overturn long-standing strongholds over regions.

The Definition of Revival

There are some challenges in the quest for revival. It is a term that many find themselves dumbfounded to define, while others have given up hope of ever seeing revival come. The argument over definition is a great obstacle to revival in our time. The word *revival* comes from a Latin word meaning "live again" and carries the idea of restoring something to normal. Spiritual revival is essentially returning to God's original intention for normal Christianity. *Chadhash* is the Hebrew term from which we get revival—it means newness, a new genesis, a new paradigm, a new song. An awakening brings a new song to the forefront of the heart. In revival, the Holy Spirit takes our mindsets, priorities, and worldviews and brings them back to the vintage intention of the Kingdom.

Revival, in its truest essence, is the manifest power of God lifting humankind to the proper standard of supreme life and righteousness. Revival occurs when God reveals His mind to us regarding His ideal vitality for His Body in the earth. A revival is a revolt against anemic, watered-down, knock-off Christianity. A revival is essentially an unfiltered and unadulterated manifestation of God. Revival raises the trajectory of your expectancy and spiritual aspirations to higher glory. It creates a longing for more of His power and character to manifest in your life at unprecedented levels. Revival is bringing to completion everything promised in the divine purpose of God in order for His people to see full restoration. Revival is never being satisfied to park the car of your walk halfway up the mountain.

Revival is the passion for daily crucifixion of the self-life. It is getting on your knees and pouring out your soul on behalf of others. Revival is operating from a vantage point of heavenly places to break darkness off of a generation. Revival is not a series of meetings people call together; man is not revival's ultimate scheduler or advertiser. Revival is not hype or human-generated programs. It's not grandstanding or mesmerizing the crowd with a carbon-copy personality. Revival is the ultimate mirroring and accurate portrayal of the heart of the Father. Revival is the pinnacle of what a Christian can experience here on Earth. So any confusion or watering down the term will cause us to lose steam in pressing into this glorious enterprise. What is revival but a triumph of light over darkness? It is the radiance of healing rather than the mangling of disease. It is spiritual aggressiveness, a move into the field of battle at a crucial time.

Revival contains the evidence of His presence. People get hungry for the raw presence of God, and then bring Him into the marketplace, leaving a tangible residue of His presence when they go. His words start leaping off your lips more freely and more often. Can I get a witness? The highest contribution an individual can make is not sitting around hoping for a corporate revival, but doing what one can to surrender the first piece of geography that revivals historically hit—the space in the left center of your chest cavity. Missionary statesman Norman Grubb says it best in *Continuous Revival*:

The truth is that revival is really the Reviver in action, and He came 2,000 years ago at Pentecost. Revival is not so much a vertical outpouring from heaven (for the Reviver is already here in His temple, the bodies of the redeemed) as it is a horizontal out moving of the reviver through these temples into the World. It is a horizontal rather than a vertical movement...[4]

We have had many types of revivals, awakenings, and reformations, all of which have propelled the Church into God-intended purposes and brought in an improbable harvest. But the revival that is on the radar will be a composite of all previous revivals combined. The Holy Spirit is saving the best for last. So get ready, emerging revivalist, for the adventure of your life!

1

Jonah Speaks Sign Language

But He answered and said to them, "An evil and adulterous generation seeks after a sign, and no sign will be given to it except the sign of the prophet Jonah. For as Jonah was three days and three nights in the belly of the great fish, so will the Son of Man be three days and three nights in the heart of the earth" (Matthew 12:39-40).

One thing that stands out about revivals is that no two of them are alike. Each revival differs based on the vessels God chooses and the backdrop of their culture. Going after revival is a little like hunting an animal you've never seen (this generation hasn't witnessed a sweeping revival) and only having a loose list of its tendencies. However, we are given an experienced Guide (Holy Spirit) and a manual of complete instructions (Holy Bible).

One day, after slapping an eviction notice on some demons by setting a demon-possessed, blind, mute man totally free, Jesus was accused of being on the side of darkness by religious folks. After

Jesus explained that deliverance could only be accomplished by the Kingdom of God coming upon the man, the religious leaders had the audacity to ask for a sign—as if the walking token of a seeing, talking, and demon-free man wasn't enough. Jesus' works were signs that God's Spirit was in Him and that God's Kingdom had come to man. The Pharisees saw miracle after miracle and still did not want to believe. So Jesus identified them as an *"evil generation."*

This text has often been misused to support the notion that God opposes releasing signs in our midst. This angle twists the original intent so much it gives it a hernia. Every generation demands a spiritual reality. The more secularized a society, the more people will hunger for the supernatural. What Jesus emphasized here is just the opposite—signs will always be given to authenticate and direct honest seekers and even the most darkened generation. In fact, Jesus declared that the *"sign of Jonah"* would specifically be utilized, even amidst evil times:

> *And while the crowds were thickly gathered together, He began to say, "This is an evil generation. It seeks a sign, and no sign will be given to it except the sign of Jonah the prophet. For as Jonah became a sign to the Ninevites, so also the Son of Man will be to this generation"* (Luke 11:29-30).

What is this sign, and what does it mean to our generation? The answer to that is one of the keys to seeing an outpouring. Luke brings up an interesting twist: *"Jonah **became** a sign to the Ninevites."* Jesus could have compared Himself to the Hebrews breaking out of Egyptian bondage, to Daniel coming out of the lion's den, or to any unbelievable restoration. But He chose a reluctant prophet who was vomited up on a beach after a 72-hour ride in a big fish. The phrase *"Jonah **became** a sign"* is a revelation that I believe the Spirit of God is reproducing in His people in order to fulfill His end-time purposes. In this hour, more than you being an instrument to release signs to this generation, God is going to release you to be a sign to this generation. When a vessel gets miraculously morphed into a sign, all bets are off. Heaven tips a historic scale in favor of an unbelievable influence and invasion. That invasion has the potential to trigger a mass response toward the Kingdom that constitutes an awakening. The term "stacking" refers to throwing up a gang sign. You might say that God is stacking things in favor of righteous reformations, a historical ingathering, and a ganging up on darkness.

As John declared:

*Love has been perfected among us in this: that we may have boldness in the day of judgment; because **as He is, so are we in this world*** (1 John 4:17).

God has some serious designs to reproduce His Son through you and me. Jesus was a sign to His generation and so you too will be in this age. God will see to it that the world will continue to encounter Jesus through revived Christianity. We are God's visual aid to the earth—we are to demonstrate His nature.

Here is the initial account of Jonah:

Now the word of the Lord came to Jonah the son of Amittai, saying, "Arise, go to Nineveh, that great city, and cry out against it; for their wickedness has come up before Me." But Jonah arose to flee to Tarshish from the presence of the Lord. He went down to Joppa, and found a ship going to Tarshish; so he paid the fare, and went down into it, to go with them to Tarshish from the presence of the Lord (Jonah 1:1-3).

The prophetic always plays such a strategic part in awakenings and summoning revivalists to live in sync with Heaven. When God speaks, it's an event; something is birthed. Yet a vessel must be yielded and positioned to be launched. Jonah came from a rather obscure part of Israel. Many could have wondered, "What could rise out of that isolated region?" But annals of history are filled with the fact that often God does the very thing people least suspect. In fact, the unusual, the unpredictable, and the unlikely become par for the course in revivals. God often *zigs* when you're thinking *zag.*

Losing the Notion
That Contradicts His Motion

Andrew Murray was a champion of the South African Revival of 1860. As a youth his family had moved from Scotland to South Africa to become missionaries. Andrew's father prayed for revival and read accounts of great historic moves of the Spirit to his family. Following this, he poured out his heart with tears to God for a similar outpouring on South Africa. This marked Murray as a young man, as did his exposure to the miracle ministry of Johann Blumhardt. Murray went to Germany to visit this ministry and witnessed healings and deliverances, convincing him that greater power was available to the Church than many believed. You are of no use to anyone if you do not have fresh awareness of the realm of the Spirit. He went to Scotland for schooling, and during graduate school became affiliated with Het Reveil, a movement that stood against the tide of popular rationalism and focused on revival. Then Murray returned to South Africa to become a pastor, yet in time grew dissatisfied. He wrote:

> When I look at my people, my peace forsakes me. I am forced to flee to the Master to seek a new and more entire surrender to His work. My prayer is for revival, but I am held back by the increasing sense of my own unfitness for the work…Oh, that I may be more and more a minister of "the Spirit."[1]

The Lord dealt with Murray on an ongoing basis that made him thirsty for living water. But the young minister still had some misconceptions on how revival would come and expected that the Holy Spirit would move through preaching and the pastor (him).

God was going to humble Andrew Murray by sending a revival for which he wasn't the primary catalyst.

The South African churches were desperate, and in 1860 they put on a conference to discuss revival and begin united prayer for a move of the Spirit. God did not keep them waiting very long. J. Edwin Orr, a revival historian, writes in *The Fervent Prayer* that in Worcester, South Africa, an outbreak of the Holy Spirit came among 60 young people gathered in a hall, being led in intercession by an assistant to Murray. Several requested the singing of a hymn, and some offered a prayer. When a Fingo girl asked if she could do the same, permission was hesitatingly granted. (Fingos were the lowest class.) While she was praying, a noise like a rolling thunder was heard, shaking the whole place. Everyone spontaneously burst into audible prayer, aware of this unusual outpouring of the Holy Spirit.

Andrew Murray, upon finding scenes of chaos, tried to shut it down, thinking it was out of order, but couldn't get them to be quiet. He left angry and confused. Later, he got before the Lord and the Holy Spirit assured him that it was of God. Murray then humbled himself and let God move the way He wanted. Subsequently, Andrew Murray was greatly used of God in spreading the outpouring throughout his nation. Lives were changed and holiness became popular. The revival raised up so many leaders that it answered the crisis of a nation that had previously been godless. The revival shook the entire countryside, and all classes were equally impacted. It didn't just stick to the populated areas, but it was felt in areas where there was no outside contact. People were frequently gripped with intense conviction. Strong men sobbed, while others fell to the ground and had to be carried out of the meetings, but were born again!

Who would have guessed that a young, female Fingo peasant would take the microphone and her place in the history of revivals?

When the World Pulls the Blankets Off

Jonah lived under King Jeroboam II in the Northern Kingdom, whose regime was rebellious. Jonah had a rebellious streak and might have been influenced by his culture. Nineveh was an intimidating place to go. This Assyrian capital was the largest city in the world at the time (estimated population of 1.5 million), and its people were ruthlessly violent. They flayed people alive and kept stacks of their victims' skulls. They were well-known for their brutalities and idolatries.

Jonah was either hardened to the possibility of a favorable response by Nineveh or calloused to their dangerous position before God. He ran from his destiny, delaying revival by placing his own plan ahead of God's divine script. You can't advance the Kingdom with people who are in retreat!

Jonah left his assignment and boated in the opposite direction to Tarshish. When a storm came to bring everything down, the heathen sailors began to cry out to their pagan gods. Everybody was in "prayer mode" but Jonah:

> *But the Lord sent out a great wind on the sea, and there was a mighty tempest on the sea, so that the ship was about to be broken up. Then the mariners were afraid; and every man cried out to his god....But Jonah had gone down into the lowest parts of the ship, had lain down, and was fast asleep. So the captain came to him, and said to him, "What do you mean, sleeper? Arise, call on your God; perhaps your God will consider us, so that we may not perish"* (Jonah 1:4-6).

We must have passion greater for our God than the world's passion for their idols. I've had this thought: *Eliminate the sleeper and you eliminate the storm.* That storm wasn't there because of wicked sailors; it was there because a rebellious prophet was sleeping on his divine assignment of a city takeover.

Sometimes it takes storms in life to awaken God's people to the reality that eternity is at stake. These modern storms include natural disasters, violence, war, terrorism, child abuse, family breakdowns, suicide, and chemical addictions. We can choose to pretend that we are asleep, lower the trajectory of our faith, and dock in a watered-down version of Christianity. Or we can wake up.

Runaway revivalists jeopardize more than those in their boat. There's the potential of missing being at the forefront of a move by ignoring God's voice. We must say yes to the reviving presence of the Lord and understand the power of light we are packing. D.L. Moody heard the words of British revivalist, Henry Varley, who said, "The world has yet to see what God will do with a person who is fully consecrated to Him!" D.L. Moody's response was, "I will do my utmost to be that person."[2] God is waking His people up in time for them to strategically place themselves as solution-centers who are able to expose the nakedness of false beliefs.

As Jonah was napping, the "unsaved" sailors rebuked him for sleeping and not calling on his God. Jonah must have felt "fingered," because they sensed he knew the cause of the trouble. Often, God comes in His mercy and pulls the blankets off rebellious revivalists on the run. Maybe the world's frustration with us is that we aren't preoccupied with what is supposed to be our preoccupation. The luxury of catching Zs instead of catching the wave of God's Spirit will no longer be afforded us. The storm has gotten too bad, and the world has become too anguished. God won't let you doze on your destiny and will even use the world to wake you up.

Heaven Is Throwing Its Sign Up

I believe that God is reaching deep into your life to pull something out. When darkness grows darker, the light of Christ in you should be glowing brighter. As we draw closer to the curtains closing on this age, demonic activity will be seeking to manifest the fullness of what the enemy has planted within man. We can also expect the greatest Christians ever to live to come to center stage in this season. The reason so many Christians look for thrills outside of Christianity is that their Christian walk is too tame. Mike Bickle of IHOP says, "We will witness God change the expression and understanding of Christianity in one generation."[3]

God intends that there be a sign representing the reality of the Kingdom. A sign is a distinguishing mark, a miraculous token or proof. God's sign will not be stopped; it may be spoken against, but it will achieve its purpose. Jonah became a sign, and like every sign, he had his setup. A sign may be swallowed up by its circumstances, even buried by impossibilities, but it will rise again. A sign is the supernatural substance of truth that transcends our explanation. Before God does any significant move in history, He first raises up a testimony (see Ps. 78:5-7). This living epistle becomes a sign to those to whom he or she is sent.

Characteristics of a Sign

A sign is called to exhibit a Kingdom characteristic before the lost world.

Revivalist Duncan Campbell once said, "A Christian is a supernatural being who has had a supernatural experience...."[4] A sign points to a reality greater than itself; signs are used to point people to their intended destination. A sign is a prototype of revived humanity.

A sign has a life that transcends the age in which he or she lives. We're supposed to bring eternity to people—not just the concepts, but also the experiences. Presenting the Kingdom of God as if it is merely principles is misleading. Earthly rhetoric can be blown off, but heavenly reality is a force to be reckoned with. The world needs to see some finished products of God's promises. A sign can't be explained by the circumstances from which it arose:

He grew up before him like a tender shoot, and like a root out of dry ground. He had no beauty or majesty to attract us to him, nothing in his appearance that we should desire him (Isaiah 53:2 NIV).

Isaiah prophesied that Jesus (the ultimate Sign) was a tender shoot. Dry ground is neither the proper ingredient for a young plant nor the optimal circumstance (hard soil) for breakthrough. But signs, by definition, have the backdrop of impossibility surrounding them.

A sign embodies a prophetic statement to a specific people. This happens when the emerging revivalist is so transformed through the Lord dealing with him or her that it marks this vessel and all who come in contact with this living sign. Living signs refuse to be reflector devices of their fallen culture or Xeroxes of pop philosophies.

Signs become passionate and tenacious to be "doors" for Heaven's resources. They seek fullness and learn to run *with* God's presence. A living sign lives a life that puts a distinction between what a man can do and what God alone can do. We will never tap into all that God has for us by copying the unrevived lifestyles of the compromised and status quo. We are His gates through which Heaven transforms Earth.

A sign maintains the core belief that God's limitlessness will show up and show off, wherever. The devil works to get a vessel to doubt his or her effectiveness in tough surroundings. Many revivalists lie dormant for a season, often due to resistance and setbacks. Yet, God always proves that demonstrations happen when what was once dormant gets detonated. God wants to use your life as evidence of the unseen realm, supernaturally illustrating truth in the midst of lies and counterfeits. God wants you to walk in a relentless mentality of expectation and extreme faith.

The Responsibility of Revival and Reformation

In the year that King Uzziah died, I saw the Lord sitting on a throne, high and lifted up, and the train of His robe filled the temple. Above it stood seraphim; each one had six wings: with two he covered his face, with two he covered his feet, and with two he flew. And one cried to another and said: "Holy, holy, holy is the Lord of hosts; The whole earth is full of His glory!" And the posts of the door were shaken by the voice of him who cried out, and the house was filled with smoke. So I said: "Woe is me, for I am undone! Because I am a man of unclean lips, and I dwell in the midst of a people of unclean lips; for my eyes have seen the King, the Lord of hosts." Then one of the seraphim flew to me, having in his hand a live coal which he had taken with the tongs from the altar. And he touched my mouth with it, and said: "Behold, this has touched your lips; your iniquity is taken away, and your sin purged." Also I heard the voice of the Lord, saying: "Whom shall I send, and who will go for Us?" Then I said, "Here am I! Send me" (Isaiah 6:1-8).

King Uzziah's death marked a significant change in the history of Israel. This was a time of what seemed to be utter disintegration in the nation—the society had turned from God, facing an obvious shift in government. Isaiah was called to minister in this time of perverted values, but before he could pursue national reformation, he had to have a personal revival. He had to be restored from his own *"unclean lips"* before he could use those lips to call the nation to the same restoration. Isaiah understood that his personal revival had given him a voice and made him a living sign of the very restoration God intended to release to Israel, and he didn't hesitate toward this greater purpose.

Our modern culture has seemingly become a pageant of ancient history, for we are a *"people of unclean lips."* Like Isaiah, we must behold a fresh revelation of the Father's glory and become radically transformed and internally equipped to extend the Kingdom.

This discovery of the encounter realm freed Isaiah from looking at the wrong things. He not only got a revelation of sin; he got a revelation that he must receive God's righteousness rather than trying to establish his own. You and I must also walk in these dimensions, for Church history tells us that humans have a bad habit of bypassing grace and trying to be righteous through their own efforts. Grace discovery is always revolutionary, as Martin Luther recognized while laboriously climbing up Pilate's staircase, trying to win righteousness by his own works. Suddenly, he heard a voice say, "The just shall live by faith." Luther got up from that encounter and launched the Reformation that began to recover the modern Church back to biblical standards.

In order to carry the revelation God seeks to birth through you to your generation, you, like Isaiah, must have: 1) a spirit of readiness, 2) a spirit of reliance, and 3) a spirit of resolve. A spirit of readiness requires a willingness to obey, as well as the responsibility to be in position, to be quickly dispatched into an assignment. A spirit of reliance requires that you understand that what God is calling you to do is humanly impossible. You must learn to trust the Lord, not lean upon your natural abilities. Finally, a spirit of resolve will be required, because, without it, the resistance and opposition will outlast you. There must be a determination to scale the mountains the Lord calls you to take, to shine the light, and to be the salt despite what hell may throw at you. You stand before a threshold, which, should you walk through, will place a demand upon your will. But if His will is your will, it will end up being darkness that backs off of your workplace, campus, loved ones, and quite possibly, your nation.

End-Time Closers

Though I never played baseball competitively after junior high, I've always loved the drama of one position: the "closer." Closers are the relief pitchers trotted out at the end of the game when everything is on the line. Closers are after only one meaningful statistic: a "save." A save means getting the opposition out and preventing them from scoring or taking the lead. Winning a close game typically motivates each team to put their best forward, particularly situational pinch hitters, so the closers that face them must be mentally tough. Closers need ice water in their veins to rise up in the midst of intense pressure and focus on getting the batter out. But closers love the responsibility of doing all they can to get a mark in the win column. They want to be on the field. That's why, when it comes close to them being called upon, you can see them stirring up their gifts, warming up by throwing in the bull pen. They're lighting a fire in the corner.

Heaven is currently calling God's "closers" to strike darkness out on an unprecedented harvest field, ushering in a dramatic "save." In America, approximately 200 million people do not go to church, many of them have never darkened a church building. As Matthew Simpson, a bishop and confidant of President Lincoln said, "Our strong [men and] congregations are fruits of revivals; and ten years without these special refreshings would show a positive decline in the churches."[5] We need something to trigger an awakening in this nation, something that arrests the soul of a wayward people. Never before have the stakes been so high and the need so great for global revival, especially since the greatest number of people ever to live are on Earth right now.

When a baseball game is close, some fans head to the parking lot before the game is over, negatively anticipating a loss because it looks bleak for their team. Today, we have Christians heading to the parking lot, not believing that we will see a save in this hour. But I'm convinced that the greatest ingathering of souls this and every other nation has ever seen is about to be unleashed. You and I are called upon and raised up for such a time as this.

It Comes With the Rain

In the classic book by Henry C. Fish, *Handbook of Revivals*, he has a chapter entitled "Revivals the Hope of the World." Written in 1874, this statement still stands. There's no question that, from history's perspective, great spiritual advances have been made in seasons of great outpourings.

Undoubtedly the granddaddy of all revivals is in Acts 2, the outpouring of the Spirit on 120 believers in the upper room. This was the flashpoint of all revivals—everything beforehand led up to this and everything that followed happened because of this. As this miraculous fire came from Heaven, the disciples spoke by supernatural utterance. Peter, who prior to the outpouring had denied Jesus, stood proclaiming the Word. Scripture recorded that about 3,000 folks were saved that day! This launched the Church as a supernatural missionary movement. All of a sudden, lame people were walking, shadows were healing folks, the dead were raised, extraordinary miracles were taking place, and regions were rocked for the Kingdom.

One of the immediate features of this revival is the extreme spiritual makeover it performed on the previously AWOL apostles. These emerging revivalists were transformed into people of conviction with holy audacity. Arthur Wallis says, "Again and again the history of revival has been the history of God's intervention to retrieve what was hopeless."[6] Though this city still hosted the dark memory of Christ's last breath, they had seen Jesus ascend, heard His promise of coming power, and now saw its extraordinary fulfillment. As out of control as things seemed, God was in control, and these were the signs of His divine order. The exploits of that day showcase the reality and importance of revivals. The festival of Pentecost brought multiple thousands of people into Jerusalem, and Heaven seized the moment. Pentecost was but one partial fulfillment of a larger preview of coming attractions. This revival made the movement, made the apostles, and launched Christianity into the known world.

Peter stood up to give an answer to the questions and confusion of the onlookers and began by citing the prophecy of a minor prophet: *"...this is that which was spoken by the prophet Joel"* (Acts 2:16 KJV). Though spoken centuries earlier, God breathed on and honored His Word. All revivals have their origins in Scripture and are a fulfillment of the Word. It is also clear that revivals come through someone laying hold of the promises and activating them. If your experiences are below His promises, it should call forth a holy pursuit. The message spoken by Peter lasted a few minutes, yet the result was the greatest forward movement for Christ up to that time. The multitudes who had heard Christ, and were unwilling to commit, repented in the Jerusalem Revival.

In the Day of Thy Power Revisited

Arthur Wallis impacted the United Kingdom and the world with his revolutionary teachings. Wallis was deeply impacted by the accounts of (The Ulster) Revival in 1949, which he preached at with an emphasis on the work of the Holy Spirit. In 1956, he wrote a classic book on revival entitled *In the Day of Thy Power*, in which he emphasized two components revival addresses: 1) revival counteracts spiritual decline, and 2) revival creates spiritual momentum.

Counteracting Spiritual Decline

The second law of thermodynamics, also called the law of entropy, means that systems left to themselves without the input of energy tend to dissipate. Entropy is also defined as inevitable social decline and degeneration. Revival is the divine moment when God bursts on the scene and reverses this decline with an intervention of His power.

By the time of Pentecost, the religious order of the day was one of outward laws and conformity. The Jerusalem outpouring launched a crisis intervention and brought life to the early Church. From that point on, a spiritual juggernaut was released and refused to be stopped. The Church thrived in persecution, and the blood of the martyrs only served to propel her. An outpouring empowers us to stare down intimidation.

Then in the fourth century, Constantine became Roman Emperor. He embraced Christianity and made it the official religion of Rome. This brought political religion into that generation, rather than people led by the Holy Spirit, and decline resulted. We see this in modern culture whenever Christianity becomes a faddish pop culture affiliation rather than a consecrated, passionate life conviction. This waters down the 100-proof righteous standard required to turn a nation around.

After a while, believers failed to walk in the light they had received and lapsed into lifeless formality. The Church fell headfirst into the Dark Ages and seemed to be off life support. She had no pulse until the 14th century came with the "Morningstar of the Reformation," John Wycliffe. Wycliffe translated the Bible from the Latin Vulgate to English, seeking to bring the light of the Word to every man. This paved the way for Martin Luther and the Reformation, and each revival has successively counteracted the spiritual decline. Desperate times demand Heaven's intervention, and on the stage of history, desperation has always been the vehicle of revival.

Creating Spiritual Momentum

Arthur Wallis wrote:

There is another well-known military principle known as concentration of force, according to which a commander will husband his reserves, concentrate them at a strategic point, for a vital blow at the crucial moment. He will thus hope to break through the enemy defenses and so produce momentum or advance where all was static.[7]

Revivals not only counteract spiritual decline; they also press the Kingdom pedal to the metal and accelerate the purposes of God. Darkness really has no defense when God releases an extraordinary move of His Spirit. Revivalists see an in-breaking of the Kingdom. As the Kingdom comes, it brings with it signs of God's rule. Heaven signals to the powers of darkness that the beginning of the end has come for them. This is an amazing moment in history, a moment when the power of Heaven is being restored to the Church. This concentration of force breaks open regions and hearts. Once it is released, it spreads like a holy plague that infiltrates every area of a culture. It's interesting that the same Sanhedrin that got the disciples to hide and hush up (revivals are primarily held back by religious systems) couldn't shut up these same men after the outpouring, or shut them out of the mainstream. Revivals seem to do that.

Signing Off on the Revelation

Jonah begins where all historic awakenings begin and that is with a revelation that comes from God. The Word of the Lord came to him, but he didn't run with it; he ran from it.

There's a fresh stirring arising in the hearts of God's people downloading in them a desire to aggressively pursue a move of God. Every believer makes a choice; every church makes a choice. When God does something fresh, a new container is needed for it, and there's always the danger of living out of old experiences.

The first step in becoming a sign is signing off on the revelation that you have received. In other words, you must abandon yourself to the divine directive given. Until this requirement is met, you cannot step into the miracle in motion.

Some years ago, I received a unique revelation in the form of a dream. I dreamt that I was riding in a car with James Ryle, who then pastored a church in Colorado. He turned and prophesied that I would see three things: 1) an outpouring of the Spirit; 2) an armory of spiritual weaponry (this generation); and when I woke up, I could not recall what the third thing was. Knowing that this was a God dream and that I only had two-thirds of the revelation bothered me for months. During that time, I found myself ministering at the University of Colorado and realized that I was in James Ryle's city. I had to find out, so I called his church and explained my dilemma to his secretary, fully expecting to be blown off as weird. Ten minutes later, to my surprise, I got a call from James and he invited me to join him for lunch.

When I got there, I could not believe that I got in to see James Ryle. As I explained my dream to him, he began to prophesy to me that I would see a massive outpouring of the Spirit, an armory of lethal believers raised up, and a Jesus movement in His Glory. Then he proceeded to give a Scripture passage that possesses all three components of my dream (see Isa. 33:16-17). I left his office that day shaking, yet sensing that God had something for me to partner with Heaven on that would radically alter my life. I said yes that day, and I still carry the same affirmation in my heart. I now realize that this is the historical stuff that awakenings are made of, and I am convinced that I will see this.

As I close this chapter, I want to challenge you to step into the revelation that God has intended for your day. God wants to invite you to rewrite the script of your life for His eternal purposes, which may look altogether different from what you think. The Spirit of Revival is looking for emerging revivalists who will run with this holy mandate and not run from it. As you receive this revelation, something will grip your heart with such a glorious urgency and baptize you in a righteous abandonment. This will determine the wake of revival that you can be entrusted with. So get ready for the adventure of the ages as you dive into this journey with me. You and I are His signs to the nations!

2

Make Way for Metanoia

There is no symptom of a feeble and diseased life more terrible than we get so accustomed to it as not to believe any great change is possible.—Andrew Murray

The church will either have revival or a funeral. —Leonard Ravenhill

Repent to Start the Sequence

In revival, large numbers of people who have been indifferent to spiritual realities become intensely roused to them—beginning with Church people. Charles Finney, a great revivalist in the 1800s, said, "We can expect a revival when the sinfulness of sinners grieves and distresses Christians." As we saw with Isaiah, this holy grief flows from the conviction of our own sin and worldliness. This is why Frank Bartleman, the intercessor and journalist of the Azusa Street Revival, said, "The depth of your repentance will determine the height of your revival." The *greatest need* of this generation is that the Church would make a wholehearted return to the purposes of God.

One of the definitions of revival is to restore something to its original purpose. God's love compels Him to rescue you from activities you have no business doing; in doing that He redeems the redeemed. One of the most universal signs of revival has been the yielding of people due to dealings of God. For example, in George Whitefield's meetings during the First Great Awakening, people would spontaneously cry out and fall down at his meetings, the majority of which were outdoors. He was a *sign* as he preached to perhaps 10 million hearers on two continents. Lady Huntington, who played a large part in the revival, wrote to Whitefield about people crying out and falling down in his meetings. She advised him to leave them alone and not to remove them as he had been doing. She told him, "Don't be wiser than God. Let them cry out."[1]

The world doesn't cry out until the followers of Christ first cry out, come clean, and throw themselves into the currents of God's dealings. Emerging revivalists are given a holy understanding of their times and how crucial the hour is. J. Edwin Orr said this:

> The Church will be moved when its members are moved. Who will be one of Revival's advance guard?...We must not regard revival as some supernatural occurrence which we cannot understand. Revival for the individual is simply deeper blessing...deeper blessing is the reward for growth in grace....Thus we see the greatest tragedy of all—this paralysing, deadly backsliding is wholly unnecessary, wholly uncalled for. At any time, an individual or a church may receive "blessing that there shall not be room enough to receive it."[2]

You and I have a holy obligation to prove God's promises, and we must prove them now. Why haven't we seen a full-fledged revival yet in our day? Inconsistency hurts your ability to receive what God wants to give you. Jonah had to deal with this issue.

Even the sailors, who knew that Jonah fled from the presence of the Lord, asked him, "Why have you done this?" Jonah had a solid confession of the sovereignty of God, but it was inconsistent with his conduct. The knowledge of God must lead us to the knowledge of ourselves.

Repentance gets a lot of bad press, but repentance is really about freedom, victory, and walking in the presence of God. Repentance cancels the oppressive strategy of darkness over your life and sphere. The Greek word for repentance is *metanoia*. This word means to think differently, to change your mind or purpose so effectively that it acquires salvation for a sinner who yields. Repentance allows a vessel to be in sync with God and the mind of Christ. Bill Johnson, a modern revivalist, says, "Repent means to go back to God's perspective on reality."[3] Repentance always involves two turns—the first away from sin and the second toward God. The reward for repentance is the promise of waves of God's presence bringing a supernatural refreshing season:

> *Repent therefore and be converted, that your sins may be blotted out, so that times of refreshing may come from the presence of the Lord* (Acts 3:19).

You are meant for signs and wonders. Your destiny includes the invasion of the impossible—emptying wheelchairs, banishing cancer, and opening deaf ears. Miracles are ready to be released through you in the marketplace. But before the miraculous move makes a comeback, personal holiness must make one.

Sounds of the Congo

In February of 1953 in Congo, Africa, a revival broke out. The flashpoint that ignited the fires of revival was a decision made by the missionaries and the indigenous people to get right with God. The epicenter was Lubutu, at a worker conference for African evangelists. Pivotally, these people expressed a deep desire to meet with God. That night the Africans met alone, and suddenly the Spirit descended. Wailings could be heard from their meeting place. The revival traveled like a bushfire, spreading over hundreds of miles, impacting the entire nation. A missionary who was there, David M. Davies, said, "God is light and whenever people encountered Him and had anything of darkness in them, they were undone."[4] This revival carried a holy fire with it, and as people testified, the Holy Spirit fell on them. Believers and unbelievers alike immediately came under conviction and into right relationship with God. There were services of open confession by believers and ministers where the cries were heard outside the church. It carried such an anointing that the next day more people packed into the church and got saved. One leader said, "We have never seen anything like it before. Words fail to describe it, but we know something now of what it must have been like on the day of Pentecost."[5]

On a Friday in July 1953, 100 people attended a weekly fellowship in the Bible school in Ibambi, in the northeast province of the Belgian Congo. Jack Scholes stood to lead in prayer. Suddenly, all heard the roar of an approaching hurricane. When they went to close the wooden shutters, there were no dark clouds, no dust spirals, nothing to indicate a storm was near. Yet the building seemed to rock as if it was in an earthquake. All over the hall people were on the ground crying out for mercy and uncontrollably quaking, while others were glorifying God with radiant faces. As many were broken under conviction, coldness of heart lifted from the people and was followed by unbelievable joy and extraordinary power.

The prophetic was evident in this move. One night, the wife of an African chief elder named Pelaza had an encounter with God in her sleep. Some were awakened upon hearing her cry out, so they ran to her house and found her in an upright position in her bed shaking and thanking Jesus, continuously. She had a vision from the Lord where she saw a great light, and God spoke to her, saying, "Pelaza, I want to do a great work here, but there is much hardness. If you want to light a good fire, do you get one by laying the wood among the ashes? I want a clean place for my fire."[6] She knew that the ashes must first be removed.

That's exactly where we must begin as we contend for a darkness-shattering move of God of epic proportions. Ashes suffocate fires and eventually put them out. The Levites were commanded to keep the fire burning, which depended on taking out the ashes (see Lev. 6:11-13).

The leaders of the Congo Revival put together a holy guideline for their move:

- Is there a love for the truth, and are you sensitive to it?

- What is your attitude to a lie? Is it hateful to you?

- Are you willing, as far as possible, to put a wrong right by making restitution or asking forgiveness of the person wronged?

- Are you willing to make a public confession of the Lord Jesus?

- Does the praise go to the Lord?[7]

The people took these guidelines seriously and went to great lengths to make things right with others. Folks were asking people for forgiveness and paying back anything they took from others and releasing offenses. This revival also demolished empty ritual Christianity. In his book on the Congo awakening, *The Spirit of Revival*, Norman Grubb describes some examples of this:

> I used to pray like a parrot; now I pray with the understanding: We used to read the Word without knowing what we were reading; now it is as honey because we have received Understanding! Our relationship with wife and children is now different as light from darkness.[8]

Finally, the Congo Revival of the 1950s saw boldness and miracles after repentance. Women who were previously intimidated became "lions" of the faith.

Men who stumbled over words became statesmen, and young kids began to declare the Word publicly. A deaf woman's ears opened up as she was filled with the Holy Ghost. A little boy who had a deformed body was totally healed and people given up for dead were raised up. Many other phenomenal signs and wonders were reported.

Helen Rosevear, a veteran missionary, was interviewed about the Belgian Congo Revival in the 1950s and she shared some insights:

What was the strongest sense you had around you at the time?

Conviction of sin. People began to confess publically what you might call 'big sin.' They spoke of adultery, cheating, stealing, deceit. One friend, whom I thought too good to be true, was crying out to God for mercy and confessing her sins. I couldn't imagine she'd done anything wrong.

…How long did all this go on for?

We didn't leave the hall the whole weekend. Most of the time God was dealing with our sins. …Then, joy struck the repentant sinners and the pastors moved on. …

It was irresistible!?

Yes! There were also amazing visions of hell and people would break down weeping because of unsaved relatives. They carried exhausting prayer burdens. There were waves of outpoured prayer. Some went off at 4 AM on one occasion and walked twelve miles to a village, compelled by the Holy Spirit, to share the gospel. Many were saved as a result.[9]

Man Overboard

If you feel called to be a revivalist, a person focused on bringing supernatural flames and overturning satan's edicts in a nation, drastic measures must be taken internally first. Jonah told the sailors to pick him up and throw him in the sea to bring "calm" to their surroundings. Repentance is a radical act, but it's more than the initial confession. It must become an ongoing lifestyle. The inner history of revivals is characterized by a strong sense of dissatisfaction. The pleasures of the world fail to bring any satisfaction. People wake up to a realization that trading heavenly joys for earthly joys is a sorry trade-off with serious loss. Revival has always begun because of repentance manifested through radical obedience.

Jonah knew by an inward dealing that the great tempest was on account of his disobedience. Upon Jonah coming clean, the most phenomenal thing happened: the sailors cried out confessing God as Lord. Wait a second, weren't these sailors in the midst of hedonist idol worship just moments earlier? Maybe the world is waiting on Christians to get honest and demonstrate that Jesus is *all that*. Deep down inside, the world wants to see someone who believes in something strong enough that they'll sacrifice. The ability to lovingly push all our chips in the middle of the table will gain not only their attention, but also their hearts.

Darkness is not scared by all the church activity, as long as we don't get desperate to dive into the purposes of Heaven. Jonah took a dive, put himself at the mercy of the Father, and repositioned. The result was that the sea ceased from raging and the men feared the Lord, taking vows and offering sacrifices to the Lord. Jonah witnessed a micro-revival on the boat leading up to the macro-revival in Nineveh. Jonah 1:7-12 emphasizes the principle that you must repent to start the sequence of revival. Repentance is a prerequisite to experiencing and releasing the Kingdom of God. Satan hates the ability you have to come back into agreement with God and make the heart adjustment to be in tune with the Holy Spirit.

Halfway Covenant Must Give Way to All-the-Way Commitment

In the 17th century, the generation that feared God and settled the land had given way to one that had forgotten God and embraced immorality. Even people who went to church had become cold in their hearts and clung to forms rather than the flame. Andrew Murray said, "When the Spirit does not work in power, it is proof that another spirit has been allowed to take its place."

Church rolls started diminishing, and in response, the leading ministers of Massachusetts adopted a desperate measure called the Halfway Covenant. People who hadn't made a profession of regeneration could get all the benefits of was totally committed except for communion. The thought being that, in a low-impact commitment, visitors would feel comfortable and attendance would increase—these halfway members soon dominated the churches. The leaders of these churches got bodies but lost the presence as this compromise filtered into the ministry. It was soon regretted and seen as a horrendous mistake. The watered-down requirements got more people in the door, but reduced the flame of vital Christianity to a flickering spark.

Consequently, God raised up a revivalist by the name of Jonathan Edwards, who, in his famous sermon, "Sinners in the Hands of an Angry God," brought back a standard and consciousness of the Almighty. The result was the Northampton Revival. Around 620 halfway covenanters got right with God, including almost all the adults of the town. About 300 souls flocked to Jesus in six months. A real revival overthrows a spirit of man-pleasing and worldliness, causing a holy captivation to seize the heart of all who encounter it.

Just before Edwards' revival broke out, churches were full of nominal make-believers who went to church like it was a social club. Edwards wrote, "It seemed to be a time of extraordinary dullness in religion; licentiousness prevailed among the youth of the town." One guy said, "For a time it appeared as if God had forsaken New England."[10]

Who would have thought that God was on the verge of igniting a spiritual, soul-winning tsunami? Tragically, two young people died unexpectedly, creating an opening that Edwards seized. Edwards said, "A stirring of interest began in the young people as they suddenly seemed to come in direct touch with the realities behind the God-talk of the minister, and the interest spread to their parents."[11] This awakening was later forged into the first Great Awakening.

In this season, God is calling us back to a vintage, Book-of-Acts caliber, biblical spirituality. In seasons of revival people step out of their former lifestyles and rise to new levels. I see a generation being raised up and an emerging breed of revivalists like Edwards who will prophesy to the masses. In his book, *The Spiritual Awakeners*, Keith Hardman says:

> First: Revival is usually preceded by a time of spiritual depression, apathy, and gross sin, in which the great majority of nominal Christians are hardly different in any substantive way from members of secular society.[12]

Sociologist George Barna, who takes polls and measures Christian trends, has often released statistics revealing that Christians look very similar to the unsaved. We have lost our saltiness and need to get our distinctive flavor back. Hardman goes on to say, "Second: An individual or small group of God's people becomes conscious of its sins and backslidden condition and vows to forsake all that is displeasing to God."[13]

Tear Your Clothes—Immediately!

King Josiah *"tore his clothes"* when he heard the words of the Book of the Law (see 2 Kings 22:11). This "ripped shirt" revival set off one of the greatest spiritual resuscitations of the entire Bible. In fact, Josiah had the distinction of turning to the Lord in a way that no king had ever done before or after him. Josiah so caught a revelation of God's holy standard that it shifted him out of toleration to annihilation. All the corruption under his nose was suddenly unbearable and ignited him to holy activism.

Josiah matched and exceeded all the rival spiritual fervor and fuel in his generation. He turned in a way that shifted history. This turning involved his entire being—the young king became a burning one for a righteous reformation:

> *Now before him there was no king like him, who turned to the Lord with all his heart, with all his soul, and with all his might, according to all the Law of Moses; nor after him did any arise like him* (2 Kings 23:25).

Our challenge is to become the hinge point for a historic national transformation, but it requires us to turn to the King and burn for the King unlike any generation before us. Our consciousness of where we need to be as God's people and our total commitment to go after a standard will set the trajectory of the next move of God. Josiah turned in a palace and Jonah turned on a ship. Your geography of turning is not as significant as the velocity of your turning. Who will volunteer, like Jonah, to be thrown in the sea of humanity and become an answer to the raging storm that attacks the life that the Father holds as precious? Are you willing to make way for *metanoia* and start the sequence for a national awakening?

Why Revival Tarries in the New Millennium

Years ago, someone handed me Leonard Ravenhill's book, *Why Revival Tarries*. It had a tremendous impact on my life—it wrecked me, and still does. From cover to cover, this book is a call to an about-face and a facing up for the people of God to righteousness and a biblical standard.

The first reason revival tarries is that *we are disconnected from God's promises*. Revival has been downsized in our generation largely due to our negligence of the prophetic passages of Scripture.

> *I will pour water on him who is thirsty, and floods on the dry ground. I will pour my Spirit upon your descendants, and my blessing upon your offspring...* (Isaiah 44:3).

If we want an outpouring, God makes it clear that we must become thirsty for Heaven's outpouring and a holy redemptive flood to impact our lives and geography. Thirst is the trigger for revival. The prophet Isaiah gave us another prophetic springboard into an unfolding reality:

> *Rain down, you heavens, from above, and let the skies pour down righteousness; let the earth open, let them bring forth salvation, and let righteousness spring up together. I, the Lord, have created it* (Isaiah 45:8).

In such seasons, a divine influence drops upon us and the skies pour down righteousness. The hearts of men, which resemble the parched ground, are softened by that influence, and thus the earth opens, and the lost are truly converted. Then the lovely fruits of the Spirit appear in the virtues of a sincere and holy life and thus salvation and righteousness spring up together.

Likewise, Malachi gives us another promise upon which God's people are to stand and make supplications:

> *"For from the rising of the sun, even to its going down, My name shall be great among the Gentiles; in every place incense shall be offered to My name, and a pure*

offering; for My name shall be great among the nations," *says the Lord of hosts* (Malachi 1:11).

The prince of preachers, Charles Spurgeon said, "What He has done once is a prophecy of what He intends to do again." In Spurgeon's message, "A Revival Promise," he encouraged believers with, "You have God's Word for it; place your finger upon it; and on your knees beseech the Lord to do as He has said…He will never revoke His word."[14]

Isaiah says, *"As soon as Zion travailed, she brought forth her children"* (Isa. 66:8 NIV). As we become awakened by the promises of God to visit us, it connects us to birth those promises. Habakkuk petitioned God: *"O Lord, revive Your work in the midst of the years! In the midst of the years make it known"* (Hab. 3:2). The Bible makes it plain that God sends an outpouring to revive His people in response to faith-filled, heartrending prayers. You were born to see the discipling of the nations and a billion-soul harvest!

The second reason revival tarries is that *we have devalued its true meaning.* Many people have a faulty concept of revival that keeps them from seeing its attractiveness. God is looking for a people who are hungry for a mighty visitation of God, but darkness wants to put a bad aftertaste in the mouths of believers. The contemporary concept of revival differs greatly from the biblical reality. The biblical reality is a sovereign and sudden manifestation of the Spirit of God that miraculously changes anyone who comes in contact with it. Some people have so associated the "disorder" of revival with revival itself that God's extraordinary move is not welcomed. Tragically, some of these people mistake quietness and a controlled program with order, so that they think it is disorder when those things are absent. Proverbs 14:4 says, *"Where no oxen are, the trough is clean; but much increase comes by the strength of an ox."* In other words, if you want increase, you'll have to deal with messes.

Great revivalists and theologians like Jonathan Edwards have realized that when God pours out His Spirit in power, it will look different from our norm, precisely because our norm is the problem. We need a new norm, and that's what revival comes to do. When a seriously strong presence of the Holy Spirit manifests, He will bring a conviction and otherworldly atmosphere that often affects one's emotions and physical body. Falling prostrate and shaking are mentioned in many revival accounts, but the key must be the fruit of a transformed life and Jesus as the central obsession.

The third reason revival tarries is that *there is no revival cry*. God seems to wait until there is a cry for revival coming from a core of people. There must be prayer for the outpouring in order for the outpouring to come. The vision and heart for revival is given oxygen through the prayers of the saints. Prayer lays the groundwork for what is to come. Without this foundation, the weight of revival would squash us, or worst yet, leave us vulnerable to the judgment that also comes with God drawing near. In *The Spiritual Awakeners*, Keith Hardman write:

> Awakenings begin in periods of cultural distortion and grave personal stress, when we lose faith in the legitimacy of our norms, the viability of our institutions, and the authority of our leaders in church and state.[15]

It is in these crises that God fashions an inner compulsion to seek God and birth a revival cry. The origin of revival is God, but its agents are His people.

Zechariah described the revival cry that releases the showers of Heaven, which in turn releases the harvest: *"Ask the Lord for rain in the time of the latter rain. The Lord will make flashing clouds; He will give them showers of rain, grass in the field for everyone"* (Zech. 10:1). Our biggest problem regarding revival showers is not a lack of water but a lack of true thirst. If the Bible tells us to ask the Lord for rain (release the revival cry), then it should be one of our main occupations as end-time believers.

The fourth reason revival tarries is that *the trajectory of our expectations is so low.* God always requires His people to become expectant before He causes them to birth moves of the Spirit. The Israelites were told to send spies into the Promised Land and bring back a report. This was intended to spike the faith of God's people and get them to raise the trajectory of expectation and holy anticipation. But when the people believed a bad report, it lowered their expectation, thus removing them from the position to receive the promise and blessed inheritance. Remember when you first got saved how you believed everything as it related to the ability of God to meet every need. When the Israelites were first released from Egypt, they had a higher trajectory and "tiptoe" anticipation. In fact, they even sang about their God's dominance over the inhabitants of the Promised Land:

> *Then the chiefs of Edom will be dismayed; the mighty men of Moab, trembling will take hold of them; all the inhabitants of Canaan will melt away. Fear and dread will fall on them; by the greatness of Your arm they will be as still as a stone, till Your people pass over, O Lord, till the people pass over whom You have purchased. You will bring them in and plant them in the mountain of Your inheritance, in the place, O Lord, which You have made for Your own dwelling, the sanctuary, O Lord, which Your hands have established* (Exodus 15:15-17).

But between Exodus 15 and Numbers 13, something happened that lowered their trajectory. This illustrates many believers who have high trajectories when they are first delivered, but over a period of time allow life, disappointments, offenses, and general jadedness to dampen their expectations. We must resolve to not allow our fervor to decline from our original passionate devotion, sacrifice, and faith, because we will end up changing what a "win" looks like. We move from the meaningful target of revival to an insignificant turf of survival. Darkness has so drugged the Lord's people that it doesn't seem to bother some that no one is getting saved around them and that all the spiritual vitals speak of a diminished existence. Don't let darkness or disillusionment downsize you. A big reason that Israel's trajectory of expectancy descended between the Red Sea and the Promised Land is that they forgot their history. Had they rehearsed in their minds the history of God's deliverance and miraculous provision, they would have risen in faith and occupied the land.

Revival author James A. Stewart said:

The tragedy in the history of the Pilgrim Church on earth is that generation after generation has lived and died without even a faint glimpse of that splendor which shines through during such times of refreshing and restoration.[16]

We have a generation rising up that doesn't know how dark it has gotten before and how God intervened by sending a glorious revival. If you don't know your history, you fall into the trap of believing that it has never been this bad before and that there is no remedy to stop this plague. By reading about former refreshings, our faith is stirred and our prayer lives are revived, paving the way for fresh outpourings of the Spirit. No, it's not enough just to know the history of revival if it doesn't lead one toward a violent desire to see God do it again. It is our destiny to reap this harvest. You were created to see His manifest presence hit continents.

The fifth reason revival tarries is that *we have a deficient value for the Holy Spirit.* Many times people have missed out on the Holy Spirit's fullness due to an inadequate view of the Holy Spirit. Paul told the Corinthian church that he didn't want them ignorant of spiritual gifts (see 1 Cor. 12:1), and we can't afford to be either. The Holy Spirit is the authorizer and agent of revival, and faulty perspectives lead to faulty receiving. Faulty receiving short-circuits one's ability to walk in the fullness of the available dimension of revival.

Many times, believers are not accustomed to giving the Holy Spirit headship in their meetings, let alone their lives. But during the revival, Evan Roberts often wouldn't even get to the pulpit unless he felt the Spirit's prompting. The bottom line is that there can be no revival apart from the Holy Ghost. I have seen churches that have moved the Holy Spirit to a back room for fear they might offend first-time visitors. The only reason they do this is ignorance of what the Holy Spirit would do if He were truly let loose in His House. We need the Dove.

Acts describes the work of the Holy Spirit in Christ's life: *"...how God anointed Jesus of Nazareth with the Holy Spirit and with power, who went about doing good and healing all who were oppressed by the devil..."* (Acts 10:38). If there is any doubt of what happens when the Dove has a resting place, this passage settles it. There are many sincere Christians who are living at spiritual poverty levels because they are not aware of the "full-benefits package" called the Comforter. Part of His job description is to release all that Jesus purchased for us at the cross. The world's greatest need today is Spirit-filled people. Our generation will come to God only when it sees new demonstrations of God's reality in His people. We need God to send revival by the mighty power of the Holy Spirit and deliver us from second-rate Christianity!

3

Tipping Points and the Third Person of the Trinity

"Going viral" is a term that, well, has gone viral. It carries the connotation that something is being passed among people like a virus—or in Old Testament terms, "a plague"! Revivals always eventually go viral. In fact, it can't be called a revival without this phenomenon. Genuine revival cannot be contained by city limits, socioeconomic status, or denominational preferences. It spreads like an airborne contagion, resisting attempts to suppress, repress, or keep it in check

Before a move of God goes viral, however, there must be a tipping point. In physics, a tipping point is the point at which an object is displaced from a state of stable equilibrium into a new, dynamic state. Spurgeon says, "Revival is a season of glorious disorder." Predictability goes out the window. When God sends revival, He doesn't come to mesh into our religious routines. He comes to overtake us with this power and presence. In climatology, a tipping point is the point at which the global climate changes irreversibly from one state to a new state. In revival, Heaven seizes the spiritual climate of a region and brings a divine charge that is transforming. Malcolm Gladwell defines a tipping point in sociological terms: "the moment of critical mass, the threshold, the boiling point."[1] It's the name given to that one dramatic moment in an epidemic when everything can change all at once. A tipping point is often a turning point. I also believe that tipping points are the flashpoints in time when something goes mainstream.

Jonah had at least a couple of developments that constituted his tipping point for the Nineveh Awakening. My vote for the ultimate moment was when Jonah talked to God from the belly of the swimming beast:

> *So they picked up Jonah and threw him into the sea, and the sea ceased from its raging. Then the men feared the Lord exceedingly, and offered a sacrifice to the Lord and took vows. Now the Lord had prepared a great fish to swallow Jonah. And Jonah was in the belly of the fish three days and three nights. Then Jonah prayed to the Lord his God from the fish's belly* (Jonah 1:15–2:1).

It was the first time Jonah leaned into God's dealings and the Father's agenda for a city takeover and spiritual awakening. From this point, this "great fish" prepared by God headed irreversibly toward the beaches of Nineveh. Tipping points shift a God-seeker into the approaching phase of a move of God.

In his book, *The Tipping Point*, Malcolm Gladwell cites three dynamics that cause a phenomenon to reach a tipping point that makes it go viral: 1) The Law of the Few, 2) The Stickiness Factor, and 3) The Power of Context.[2] According to Gladwell, these are the mechanisms by which certain things achieve exponential popularity. For the dynamic of revival, I want to rename them: 1) The Carrier, 2) The Contagion, and 3) The Climate.

The Carrier

In biblical accounts of revival in the Old Testament, each one began in the heart of a consecrated servant of God who became the energizing power behind it—a Carrier. The Carrier is the individual catalyst who champions and embodies the revelation before it goes mainstream. This person connects the concept of revival to people and represents a walking Website of what Heaven wants to release. These catalysts become "super infectors" who cause God's move in its infancy to be epidemic, and eventually massively epic, as they yield to God's Spirit.

Perhaps the biggest move of miracles in the history of the Church since the Book of Acts is the Azusa Street Revival. One of the primary Carriers of this revival was an African-American man, W.J. Seymour. Seymour was the son of former slaves and became a catalyst for a movement that now includes over 600 million worldwide and is growing exponentially. Other Carriers of the Azusa Street Revival were Charles Parham and Frank Bartleman. Parham founded a school in Topeka, Kansas, called Bethel Bible School where students were pressing in for the baptism of the Holy Spirit with the gift of tongues. Through a connection, Seymour, who was desperate for more of God, went to Bethel School. Due to racism and segregation, Seymour had to fight through narrow mindsets that sought to hinder him in order to drink of the teaching on the baptism of the Holy Spirit there.

Those put into crushing circumstances, when mixed with a hunger for God, become vessels for an awakening. The best oil (anointing) comes from pressing in and desperation. After a while, Seymour received an invitation to come to Los Angeles. He went, even though he hadn't received the baptism of the Holy Spirit, and arrived in January 1906. Frank Bartleman, an intercessor and journalist, had already come to Los Angeles a year earlier. In the spring of 1905, Bartleman was given a book on the Welsh revival, and after reading it he resolved to become an instrument to promote faith for a spirit of revival. After hearing F.B. Meyers tell of the Welsh revival, Bartleman promised God his full abandonment and became convinced of an imminent outpouring. Bartleman later made contact with Evan Roberts, the catalyst of the Welsh Revival, and was challenged to believe for an outbreak of God himself. Roberts told Bartleman, "Congregate the people who are willing to make total surrender. Pray and wait. Believe God's promises. Hold daily meetings."[3] He felt that Los Angeles would be ground zero for a significant outpouring of God's Spirit.

Seymour accepted the invitation to come to L.A., but after preaching on the baptism of the Holy Spirit, he was locked out of the meeting hall on the second night. He didn't have any money, but he was invited to stay in a home on North Bonnie Brae Street. Seymour called for ten days of prayer and fasting, and the heavens broke loose. A man was healed and received the baptism of the Holy Spirit, including a prayer language. Suddenly, the power of God broke out and just about all present began to speak in tongues. Several nights later, Seymour received the baptism of the Holy Spirit.

The Bonnie Brae Street house couldn't hold the crowd, so they moved the growing meetings to a two-story warehouse on 312 Azusa Street.

The Contagion

The Gospel of the Kingdom knows no parallel when it comes to impact and infiltrate the core of one's being with extraordinary power. The history of revivals clearly illustrates that its fire spreads supernaturally from heart to heart and person to person.

In the Azusa Street Revival, once Seymour and the others moved to the warehouse, the activity of the Holy Spirit among them increased and accelerated. Spiritualists were drawn to their meetings, only to have the devils cast out of them, after which they got saved and baptized with the Holy Spirit. Word got out that God was healing at Azusa Street, and people brought the sick in droves. Seymour would direct his attention to the side of the room where there were people in cots and wheelchairs and pronounce they be healed in Jesus' name. Immediately, according to eyewitnesses, everyone would get up and walk away healed. One woman named Diane had a tumor the size of a cantaloupe on the side of her head, which shrunk and disappeared. She later went into full-time ministry.

One of the most awesome wonders, and the best advertisement for the meetings, was the fire that appeared on top of the building. Neighbors would call the fire department, only to find out that there was no natural fire. Diane went to the warehouse because she saw the flames on the building and thought she could be healed. People testified of God igniting homes with this supernatural fire all over Los Angeles, with people being saved, delivered, and baptized in the Holy Spirit. Reports said that up to 21,300 people attended the services, with as many as 800 in the warehouse at one time and another 500 hearing from the sidewalk. Cecil Robeck, a historian who wrote about the Azusa Street Revival said, "The revival reached out to the rest of the world with a rapidity that is hard to imagine. It was like a fire lit in dry tinder when nobody was looking. It exploded, scattering its sparks in every direction."[4]

By fall of 1906, the Azusa Street Revival had spread up the west coast of the United States with human firebrands from San Diego, California, to Spokane, Washington. Before 1907 rolled in, these emerging revivalists were in Denver, Minneapolis, and Cleveland, as well as in regions of the South and New York. There were even revival missionaries who made it to Africa, Mexico, Canada, Western Europe, Asia, and the Middle East.

Revivals always inspire vessels to become contagious and tenacious to blanket their world with all that God has poured out. The reports of the Azusa Street Revival caused an appetite for what God was pouring out, triggering a stream of people to come from all over to experience it. Many of those who flocked to these services could feel a Holy Ghost force field from blocks away. Crowds of people received a Pentecostal impartation and were launched and sent out with fresh fire. R.E. Davies, author of *I Will Pour Out My Spirit*, says, "Revivals often spread through contact, almost like a contagion. Individuals or groups who have experienced God's power are the means of bringing it to others."[5] Many times revivalists seem to carry it to the places they go.

Never underestimate how much influence you carry with the seed of the Kingdom you have received. The devil is always trying to keep you blinded to your supernatural ability to impact people around you, but Heaven is ready to come out of the closet through you.

The Climate

The Climate is the background, circumstances, or historical moment in which a pre-revival seed "tips" into a revolutionary, epoch-shaking dynamic. In early 1906, Los Angeles had a population of 238,000 and was growing by 3,000 residents every month. It was the nation's 17th-largest city. L.A. was linked to the rest of the United States and the world by railroads and ports. This growing city was significantly diverse ethnically and had various churches throughout the city. Around the time that W.J. Seymour arrived in L.A., many Christians had been hearing about the Welsh revival and had begun to grow dissatisfied with traditional forms of Christianity. Some began to pray for revival.

Then in April of 1906, San Francisco had a massive and historic earthquake, which brought serious devastation. The shaking was felt from Oregon to Los Angeles. Fire broke out, and the death toll rose to an estimated 300. The next day, a serious aftershock hit Los Angeles, which left people sober and afraid. Bartleman, who had been saturating the city of L.A. with Gospel tracts, was pressed to attend the warehouse and gave his first message to the crowd, which was very open in the aftermath of the quake. The setting was combustible, to say the least.

Today we have micro-outpourings in certain places, massive intercession occurring, and seemingly weekly ecological or natural disasters. One could get the feeling that maybe we are getting set up for something or set apart for something.

The Third Person of Team Trinity

The dominant force of the tipping point in revival is the person of the Holy Spirit. Though the Azusa Street Revival seemed to feature the ministry of the Holy Spirit, the Holy Spirit engineers all aspects of revival. James Stewart rightly says, "There can be no revival apart from the Holy Spirit; He is the author of every Heaven-sent movement."[6]

Many times in revival, the third person of the Trinity will get heightened recognition as a person. If we think of the Holy Spirit as an impersonal force, we will never develop a relationship with Him. If we see Him as just power, we will just try to use Him. We must see Him as our heavenly Counselor, and His wisdom must be sought out and obeyed. So often we just go with the preplanned program and miss what the Holy Spirit is attempting to do. The highest priority of those in leadership must be a continual openness to the mind of the Holy Spirit.

The Great Awakening brought back a renewed emphasis on the third person of the Trinity, specifically the Holy Spirit's work of reviving and empowering the Church for worldwide harvest (missions). Then, in the Second Great Awakening, Charles Finney emphasized prayer for an outpouring of the Holy Spirit and called attention to the baptism of the Holy Spirit, which he understood to be a post-conversion experience. Richard Lovelace, author of *Dynamics of Spiritual Life*, writes:

We should make a deliberate effort at the outset of every day to recognize the person of the Holy Spirit…We should continue to walk throughout the day in a relationship of communication and communion with the Spirit…relying upon every office of the Holy Spirit's role as counselor mentioned in scripture. We should acknowledge Him as the Illuminator of truth and of the glory of Christ.[7]

This revelation transforms a safety-proof Christian into an empowered revivalist. In revivals, many believers will get baptized in the Holy Spirit and begin to flow in the gifts of the Holy Spirit. A revival is a heightened measure of the Spirit's working, activities, and manifestations.

My strongest taste of revival to date came when I visited Argentina twice in the '90s. When I got a chance to sit down with Carlos Annacondia (a miracle revivalist), I saw fire coming out of his eyes as he talked about the touch of the Holy Spirit. Annacondia was raised up by the Lord to minister in power with great manifestations of the Spirit—healings, dramatic deliverances, and massive salvations in large outdoor gatherings. I also spoke with Pastor Claudio Freidzon and asked him, "Besides the person and working of the Holy Spirit, what revelation launched the outpouring?" He told me, "There was no revelation greater [in relationship to their revival] than the person of the Holy Spirit." I'll never forget his answer and the depth in his eyes as he answered my question. I have been on a quest ever since to discover all that the Holy Spirit could be to me and all that He would release through me.

You were designed to walk in the Spirit, and if you don't, the realities and promises of the Word of God won't be your experience. You must become acquainted with the Holy Spirit as a person to fulfill the purpose of God in your generation. Deep, lasting change occurs as we experience ongoing interactions with the person of the Holy Spirit.

The Holy Spirit's agenda is for you to become an expression of God in the earth as you yield your life to Him. Following the presence of God is what allows us to step into a historic outpouring. Jonah obviously missed out on this memo to emerging revivalists:

> *But Jonah arose to flee to Tarshish from the presence of the Lord. He went down to Joppa, and found a ship going to Tarshish; so he paid the fare, and went down into it, to go with them to Tarshish from the presence of the Lord* (Jonah 1:3).

We should always make the presence of God due north on our spiritual compass. Runaway revivalists run the risk of stepping out of nation-turning moments and into storm-brewing ones. Saying yes to the ultimate reviving presence of God is what makes the difference between coasting and hosting. Coasting Christians just ride on past momentum and others' labors, while hosting Christians seek to become radiant emitters of God's presence. Welsh theologians have said that the three great characteristics of classic revival are:

- A heartfelt desire to be free from all sin and any impurities of heart.

- A powerful impact on the wider community.

- An intense, palpable, and extraordinary sense of God's presence.[8]

The Holy Spirit's role in great moves can never be underestimated or overlooked. In seasons of revival, the Holy Spirit overwhelms people and brings freedom, deliverance, transformation, and the atmosphere of Heaven. I believe that if we start to develop intimacy with the Holy Spirit, He becomes our Friend and we will flow in all He has for us. This makes for serious instrumentality for revival, because we will be led to prayer, consecration, and activism God's way.

Five Keys to Develop Greater Intimacy With the Holy Spirit

Make a place for Him. Intimacy is such a precious and private thing that it requires a place. Setting apart a place to connect with the Spirit of God allows us to have focus and is where we create memories of communion. Claudio Freidzon, another Argentinean revivalist, told me that he gave his mornings to fellowshipping with the Holy Spirit and kept to this routine even after he began to see a measure of success.

Enjoy His presence. You won't sustain a spiritual discipline unless you've tapped into its inherent joy. Paul said, *"...the kingdom of God is not eating and drinking, but righteousness and peace and joy in the Holy Spirit"* (Rom. 14:16-17). Some only see His presence as something you experience in a special service, but He is with you always. Our times with Him should be adoration, not obligation.

Embrace His pleasures. You would never invite an important person over to your house for dinner and only serve meat if the person was a vegan. The Holy Spirit is a divine person with a personality, and He can be grieved. You need to know from the Word what pleases and saddens Him. The closer you draw to Him the more He becomes a gauge of your activities, conversation, and the company you keep.

Calibrate your environment. The personal spiritual atmosphere we set and walk in is so crucial. It attracts the presence of God, and the more His presence is around you, the more His presence will flow through you. The climates we create determine the fruit that we produce.

Embrace relationship more than feeling. The Holy Spirit is not in our lives to be an experience alone, but to lead us to divine romance. Many believers stop at an experience rather than stepping into relationship. And like all great relationships, it's important not to let it get stale and become a ritual. The Holy Spirit will progress you to new levels of communion with the Father and will use yesterday as a springboard, not as a high watermark.

A.W. Tozer, an author and preacher, said, "It was God's will that we should push on into His presence and live our whole life there."[9] You must acknowledge who the Holy Spirit is as a person in order to appropriate all that He is. Those who develop a close friendship with the Holy Spirit will see Him manifest Himself in their lives more frequently. The Holy Spirit is within you and will release the Kingdom through you to meet the needs of people. He will also help you answer the demands of the times. We need the Spirit to come in power.

Early Adopters and the Signs of Revival

According to a theory formulated by Everett Rogers called Diffusion of Innovation, there's a sociological grid with a natural bell curve that says 2.5 percent of the population are Innovators, 13.5 percent are Early Adopters, 34 percent are the Early Majority, 34 percent are the Late Majority, and 16 percent are Laggers. Early Adopters tend to buy into or try out new programs sooner than most of their peers, but they are not especially prone to taking risks. A small minority of people called Innovators play that role. These are the people most likely to conceive and develop cutting-edge methodologies and become forerunners.

Hezekiah was an Innovator. He took a great risk in setting out to transform his people, calling them to sacrifice for the Passover and requesting that their captors let them go. That took some guts! It's a sociologically proven fact that in the final analysis, these types of people establish and develop culture that shapes others. In the history of revivals, there have been spiritual Innovators who sense God releasing a new wave of His Spirit and immediately jump in with both feet, trumpeting what they sense is about to spiritually break out. These people usually got disappointed with the spiritual status quo and became desperate. Their desperation caused them to press into God and seek Him for what He wanted to release in their generation. People like W.J. Seymour, Evan Roberts, Jonathan Edwards, and others became God's Innovators in their respective moves of the Spirit.

Revival demands a core of people who will come into agreement on the front end while the fire of revival is catching on. Sociologically speaking, for any new product to be successful, it must attract Innovators and Early Adopters, so that its "diffusion" moves onto the majority. Brian Edwards, author of *Revival! A People Saturated with God*, makes this point, "However, revival will rarely begin only by the faithfulness of a few good and godly men; there will almost always be others who join in the longing and praying and preparing for revival."[9] God is calling on a new breed of emerging revivalists to see what others aren't seeing and grab hold of what Heaven is pouring out in this day.

Along with the vision of revival, Innovators carry a spiritual burden for a wide-scale outpouring upon a people. Innovators are broken over the current spiritual and moral state of things within the Church. In society, they burn to see the fame of Jesus' name raised as a banner over their land. Innovators are often initially viewed as too extreme, on the fringe, or a bit off-center. Yet, they embody a spirit of revival, which must precede any corporate revival. Revival Innovators are being summoned to pursue a new move, to re-dig ancient wells, and to challenge contemporary Christianity to occupy realms neglected for ages. Revival Innovators are not OK with living off of someone else's testimony or outpouring, but are possessed with seeing a revival of their own. They won't settle for being a virtual-reality revivalist, but contend to be one of those who gets on his or her face and occasionally skips meals for the cause. They are vintage in their zeal and feel that their time is the greatest hour in history.

Soon the Early Adopters revivalists are impacted by the spiritual spark and quickly become the core that faithfully cries out for Heaven to rain and saturate the land. These Early Adopters start spreading the word and testimonies of what God has done with others. This group possesses a different spirit, like Caleb. Innovators and Early Adopters form what has been referred to historically as a "remnant." It is at this time that Heaven's confirmation brings an indisputable conviction that the holy requirements have been satisfied and revival is underway.

The Signs Are All Pointing To...

Keep in mind that every revival has its own distinction and carries the flavor of the revelation that the Father wants restored. Yet, there are some commonalities associated with the majority of revivals.

Cultural distortion. Just before a revival breaks through to the surrounding society, people seem to lose their moral footing and feel as if the existing institutions and traditional beliefs aren't working anymore. Symptoms of the cultural rug being pulled out from under folks include increased violence, drug abuse, and suicide. Ordinary coping mechanisms often break down under this unusual stress overload. This crisis of dark fogginess, injustice, and decline of a generation's morals makes room for new light and the "steel punch" of God to break through. This can really be seen in the Jesus People movement that broke out in the late '60s, and in the first Great Awakening in the 1730s. In both situations, both generations and societies seemed out of control before God answered.

Church decline and desperation. Before revival comes, we often see believers in the Church settling into status-quo Christianity coupled with a moral laxness that causes the people of God to look like outsiders. When a church hasn't experienced a revival, it doesn't get its trajectory reset for fullness. Everything begins to get spiritually dry. Outreach is either nonexistent or ineffective, and attendance dips with the bottoming out of passion and expectancy. Bishop J.C. Ryle, author of *Christian Leaders of the 18th Century*, wrote:

> From the year 1700 to the year of the French Revolution (1789), England seemed barren of all that is really good. Christianity seemed to lie as one dead. Morality, however much exalted in the pulpits, was thoroughly trampled underfoot in the streets. There was darkness in high places and darkness in low places…darkness in the country, and darkness in the town…a gross, thick religious and moral darkness—a darkness that might be felt.[11]

J.C. Ryle observed firsthand the spiritual decline of England before a great revival broke out. It's like history repeating itself all over again even in other nations. Today the Church has gotten complacent and comfortable in America. The timing is bad, too, because our nation's current state demands a representation of Christ at His best. Again, we are somewhat less than advertised, by what we've broadcasted contrasted with how we've lived. As a result, the Church is not even considered the place for "those people," but worse, we are considered irrelevant. That's about to change! Richard Riss, author of *Survey of 20th-Century Revival Movements in North America*, said:

> In response to these conditions, many will come together for intense prayer. Very often people make serious agreements with one another to pray together regularly for a fresh outpouring of God's Spirit. This engenders an exhilarating sense of expectancy that God will move in a miraculous manner. Then, suddenly, the power of God falls.[12]

This restlessness becomes the turning point where the declining Church becomes the desperate Church. They feel the strategic timing from the Lord to play their part in changing the course of history.

Conversions and cutting-edge confirmations. Sometimes it's hard to pinpoint exactly when revivals begin and where the drought officially ends. We usually mark a revival by what happens in a prayer meeting or church service, and the common occurrence is that there are some significant conversions, demonstrating that something is shifting in the atmosphere over a region. Sometimes the confirmation is out-of-the-ordinary miracles, Holy Spirit manifestations, or multitudes being drawn to a place where the presence of God dwells. In the Hebrides Revival, led by Duncan Campbell, 600 people were irresistibly drawn to an after-service prayer meeting at three in the morning. This signaled to them that a move of God was underway. Another example of a cutting-edge confirmation was in the Congo Revival of 1953. Missionary David Davies wrote a letter to an evangelist 200 miles away telling him about the visitation. As soon as the evangelist shared the letter with his church, the Spirit powerfully hit them too.

A comeback of holiness and authoritative preaching. Frank Cooke said, "The foundation of every reformation of the Holy Spirit is the Word of God made plain to people." There are some people who refuse to let the Bible say what it says. They want it to be softer and lighter. They want the demands of Scripture to sound like options and to take out the offense of its absoluteness. But our God is a consuming fire. Ian Malins, author of *Prepare the Way for Revival*, says, "There can be no revival without a fresh awareness of the holiness of God, the depth of sin, and a deep and lasting turning back to God in repentance."[13]

Historically in genuine revivals, there is first a fresh revelation of God through the anointed proclamation of the Word, which in turn produces an awareness of the altogether otherness of God. In ages of apologetic backpedaling, the Word of the Lord sounded forth with a trumpet blast that woke up nations. Jonathan

Goforth, a Canadian missionary to China, said, "We can entertain no hope of a mighty, globe-encircling Holy Spirit revival without there being first a back-to-the-Bible movement."[14]

Right before the first Great Awakening, the Wesley brothers and George Whitefield formed the Holy Club at Oxford University. They fasted until 3:00 P.M. on Wednesdays and Fridays and studied and discussed the Greek New Testament and the classics each evening. This training prepared these men to call nations back to the God of the Bible.

The Parallel Movement Principle

Often in the advent of a mighty revival, there is also an increase of demonic activity. Isaiah prophesied that as glory arose upon God's revivalists, darkness would try to cover the generation (see Isa. 60:1-2). We see that during Moses' day, right before the Exodus revival, darkness had Egyptian magicians operating under an increased demonic anointing. Jannes and Jambres (Pharaoh's magicians) were raised up at the same time as Moses (see 2 Tim. 3:8).

In Elijah's day, Jezebel raised up the false prophetic movement of Baal. These false prophets were supposed to show up the God of Elijah and call down fire. They had mesmerized the masses, but couldn't get an answer in the showdown on Mout Carmel. Ultimately, Yahweh upstaged their god by sending fire and ending their evil reign (see 1 Kings 18). Daniel out-achieved the Chaldeans with their sorcery as he interpreted dreams and solved national crises while they fell back helpless (see the Book of Daniel). We also see that during Jesus' day, the enemy raised up a magic movement that the Magi were a part of, and King Herod wanted to fully utilize them. The Magi had seriously developed their supernatural skills, but the Babe of Bethlehem changed the enemy's strategy.

Today, as we are on a glorious brink of a mighty torrent of God's Spirit, we also have a modern parallel movement called the Indigo children. These children have been featured on national investigative programs demonstrating developed physic powers. They are touted as the next stage in human evolution, possessing paranormal abilities such as telepathy. Other alleged traits include a high IQ, a built-in intuitive ability, and resistance to authority. Darkness always tries to release a preemptive strike of counterfeiting Heaven's reality, simultaneous to Heaven's mighty release of the genuine. There can also be greater warfare on the prophetic callings upon individuals' lives before a great outpouring. This can be seen upon unbelievers and believers alike, as confusion comes in to misdirect giftings and attention.

But I believe God is raising up a signs-and-wonders movement of revival deliverers who will shake the nations with the message of Jesus Christ. They will ultimately demonstrate that our God has no peers and no competition, and that Heaven always answers with greater works. The closer we get to revival, we must recognize that imitations and counterfeits showing up should actually encourage us that we are on course for the authentic wave of God to impact a generation. Knowing this, we must discover how to blaze the trail and detonate a move of God for our generation!

4

Pulling the Rip Cord
of a Modern-Day Revival

In *Cataracts of Revival*, G.J. Morgan wrote, "In the hidden ledger of God there is a specific law where every revival works accordingly, and every law runs back to the source of all things."[1] In His infinite wisdom the Father has placed a dynamic promise, which constitutes a covenant of revival, in the book of Second Chronicles:

> *Then the Lord appeared to Solomon by night, and said to him: "I have heard your prayer, and have chosen this place for Myself as a house of sacrifice. When I shut up heaven and there is no rain, or command the locusts to devour the land, or send pestilence among My people, if My people who are called by My name will humble themselves, and pray and seek My face, and turn from their wicked ways, then I will hear from heaven, and will forgive their sin and heal their land"* (2 Chronicles 7:12-14).

In his book, *Revival Fire*, Wesley Duewel says it like this:

Thousands of times God has fulfilled the revival covenant on a region, or a nation. The more [pervasive] and total the prayer and obedience of His children, the more widespread God's outpoured revival through the power of the Spirit can become.[2]

On the heels of Solomon's dedication of the Temple, the glory of God came so powerfully that everyone was overcome by the power of God. In the midst of this, God appeared to Solomon in a night visitation and gave him a promise. Now remember, the Israelites were in a time of spiritual awakening, perhaps the high point of their history. And it was at this moment that God offered a key promise that has become our desperate hope today. God knew this promise would be needed in dark days ahead, ones in which the heavens would seem to be shut and there would be no widespread outpouring of the Spirit. These dark days would be characterized by ecological, economic, and physical devastation, as symbolized by locusts devouring the land in Second Chronicles.

Today, less than a third of this current generation has any church background.[3] Consequently, we have an epidemic of drug abuse, suicide, self-mutilation, online porn, resurgence of Wicca, anorexia, sexual perversion, abortion, prostitution, rising violence, despair, genocide, and gender bending. We can choose to remain nonchalant as the modern locusts devour our land or we can raise the trajectory of our warfare and intercession. We can harden or we can humble.

God gave Solomon and His people throughout history this covenant as an invitation to solicit Heaven for revival. Before he went to be with the Lord, Bill Bright, the founder of Campus Crusade for Christ, said:

During my 40-day fast, the Holy Spirit assured me again and again that God will send a great revival to America and the world when His people heed His call to turn to Him, according to 2 Chronicles 7:14. I am confident that this awakening will result in the greatest spiritual harvest in history.

Five Stages in the Divine Summons of Second Chronicles 7:14

Stage 1: *"If My people...."* We must be gripped by the need for extreme transformation. There's no substitute for this. Without it, we will never stretch ourselves out for the healing of our land and the saving of the lost. We live in a nation that has lost its soul, and if that doesn't break us, we may have lost a part of ours. The youth, our future, have become our immediate fear as well.

We must discover the power of holy outrage over what darkness is engineering on the national scene and in the captive hearts of a generation. Jesus walked in a holy vengeance to obliterate oppression and take out the demonic weapons of mass destruction aimed at the soul of a nation. This divine intensity ought to propel us into a place where, at all costs, we will contend for a moral awakening. The moral breakdown of our nation is like the scene of the proverbial train wreck where everyone just stares in utter amazement.

Perhaps the turning point of revival happens when people get to the point where an unshakable holy resolve is born. The phrase *"If My people"* emphasizes that an individual life and a corporate body are capable of producing a nation-healing movement. Many believe that the circumstances of their nation have become too oppressive, but oppression has always been the making of revolutionaries. When God looks over a nation to evaluate its standing, it is based upon what His people are doing. God's criteria to release mercy upon a nation is based on His people emerging and identifying themselves as a chosen people:

> *But you are a chosen generation, a royal priesthood, a holy nation, His own special people, that you may proclaim the praises of Him who called you out of darkness into*

His marvelous light; who once were not a people but are
now the people of God, who had not obtained mercy but
now have obtained mercy (1 Peter 2:9-10).

Identity is huge in the Kingdom of God. Mistaken identity is the source of so many spiritual problems. All anyone has to do is to check out the Facebook page, Myspace, or "Tweets" of your average Christian young adult today. One day they're casting their vote for abandonment to the Desire of the Ages; the next day their vote is a representation of the other side. Memo: you can't click the "Like" button for both sides.

We must come to see ourselves as God sees us. In an effort to identify with the world, many churches have lost their identity as nation-disciplers. True biblical Christianity is not a passing fad modeled after the latest cultural trends is but gloriously timeless.

Seek to find out exactly how God has hardwired you. When you have an idea of who you are and the person God is making you to be, then you begin to live life large for Him. There's a divine designation upon this generation. You were meant to be God's designated cleanup hitter, batting cleanup and swinging for the fences for a Kingdom eruption to defeat darkness in the bottom of the ninth. You carry the markings of one set apart for special use.

Revivals typically begin with those who are truly closest to God. Spiritual identity crises usually give way to spiritual identity theft. Once I was involved in a faith week at a secular college. My part was to preach and at the end of the week, give an invitation at an outdoor nighttime rally in front of the dorms. The faith week began with a town-hall-style, nonconfrontational debate with representatives from different "spiritual" organizations. I decided to take this in and see how things would go.

The panel included a Wiccan student president, a Pagan Student Association representative, and a Christian leader of a historical denominational campus group. I started interceding for the Christian representative. The female Wiccan president talked about how they stood for power and how they use their powers to change their world and even affect the White House (ambitious, to say the least). Then the male pagan student leader talked about brotherhood and universal love and acceptance and how much ground they had gained recently.

Finally, the Christian representative spoke. His posture spoke of being defeated in the warm-up room. He talked about their 12-member group trying to survive as believers on campus. Now, there's nothing wrong with 12 people—Jesus turned the whole world upside down with that number. But it was as if this Christian group had set their goal on just making it through the year. I remember distinctly hearing the Lord whisper to my heart, "In this season, you can't let darkness steal our proclamations and practices." This was spiritual identity theft right before my eyes.

The Wiccan and pagan groups were talking about power to transform and a bond of brotherhood that attracted commitments, while the Christian talked about survival. It was as if they were declaring what the Christian guy should have been declaring and the Christian guy was saying what they should be saying. I walked away convicted that if we don't walk in our identity, someone will try to take it and use it against us. Recognizing who we are, and getting a revelation of what we can accomplish as God's people, is the first major step to a national awakening.

Stage 2: *"Who are called by My name...."* Make no mistake— you have been called out. You and I have been summoned by God to play a significant part in becoming catalysts for a move of God. The phenomenon of spiritual awakening, whether in Scripture or more recent history, usually begins with unlikely individuals rising to the challenge of the times in which God put them. Before a train can move, there must be a driving force. Before a rocket will launch, there must be something that puts the propulsion in the boosters. God knows how to create a spark and light a fuse, a prophetic vision, that triggers the intended vessels into a holy combustion.

Jonah was called by his name to play a major role in the Old Testament's first and only foreign missions endeavor. Had it not been for the merciful and persistent heart of the Father, the Book of Jonah would have been a classroom on what not to do! Brian Edwards, author of *Revival! A People Saturated with God*, said, "Those whom God uses in leadership in revival are always men who have met with God in a powerful personal way and have a burning passion for the glory of God...."[4] These leaders are recognized not only as creators of movements, but also as mouthpieces of movements. Being *called by His Name* also frequently comes with some heavenly distinction, an encounter where the individual knows that God is on the other line. This gives an undeniable sense of call and fuel for the movement.

In 1990, I got married and pioneered a campus ministry with my bride at what had been named the number one party school in America. Barb and I moved from her hometown to Chico, California, to attend California State University, Chico. We saw God move on this campus known for radical parties so that it became a place where people got radically saved. We had a young man come to our home Bible study high on marijuana, only to get saved and baptized in the Holy Spirit in one fell swoop. He lost his false high and got caught up in the Most High. In six short years, Chico went from being ranked the number one party school in America to falling out of the top couple hundred.

Our summons happened while watching a CNN report on "Pioneer Week," a spring break annual rite in Chico where students came from all over to party, drink, hook up, and act immorally. At the time, I was the campus pastor at the University of the Pacific in Stockton, California, where I had graduated. I thought that whoever would go to Chico State to start a ministry would have to be 51/50 (certifiably crazy). The hierarchies of devils were numerous, and they were seriously packing (as in carrying heavy artillery) in Chico.

All of a sudden, in the midst of the news report, I sensed God draw me to the lost crowd in the streets. God was showing me that He was relocating my heart and ministry elsewhere. God gave me a sense that we would be part of something special if we obeyed. I will never forget the outpouring and the lives that were changed. Make no mistake about it, you have the finger of God pointed at you and it will cost you something to see the Kingdom increase.

Stage 3: *"...will humble themselves..."* This stage is so pivotal. If skipped, there is no point in asking for revival in prayer. Mario Murillo, an American revivalist, says:

> You stand before the greatest door in history. Beyond this door lie the most precious gifts of God. Beyond this door you will find the keys, the secrets of the heroes of faith who have gone before you. They shook their generations; they established justice and they stood at one time where you now stand.

He goes on to say, "This door is not opened by talent...nor mental prowess; it is opened by an attitude."[5] The attitude that gains entrance to the greatest door in history is humility. No plan will bail us out if we lack humility before the throne of God. Proof that someone is a seeker of revival is that he or she is truly humbling him- or herself. Revival is a work of the Holy Spirit that requires the grace of the Father to operate in our midst, and this requires surrender. Isaiah prophesied that God dwells with the contrite:

> *For thus says the High and Lofty One Who inhabits eternity, whose name is Holy: "I dwell in the high and holy place, with him who has a contrite and humble spirit, to revive the spirit of the humble, and to revive the heart of the contrite ones"* (Isaiah 57:15).

Contrite comes from a Latin word that means to "grind down, to wear away." Revival comes to those who have allowed self-centeredness to be ground down and worn away.

Once we got to Chico State University, I had an encounter with the Holy Spirit on campus. The Father, in an instant, gave me His broken heart for the lost students that packed the Student Union building that day. After walking to my '79 Toyota while sobbing uncontrollably, I sat in the car and God spoke to my heart: *"Unless a kernel of wheat falls to the ground and dies, it remains only a single seed. But if it dies, it produces many seeds"* (John 12:24 NIV). I knew that brokenness was attractive to Heaven and that the Father would send life to a spiritually dead campus. Perhaps one of the biggest things He stressed to me was that I wouldn't operate on my own strength. True empowerment only comes through total identification in Christ.

Tell the Lord that you are willing to lay it all down at His feet—your future, your resources, what others think about you, and ultimately your life. Ask Him now to fulfill His promise to revive you and pour out His Spirit.

Stage 4: *"...pray and seek My face...."* Humility must create such a habit of reliance in our lives that we find ourselves on our knees. After my '79 Toyota brokenness experience, the first thing I found myself enjoying was praying. I had always had my own quiet time with God, but this was different. I was delighted in sharing the Father's heart and seeking God's face for a corporate outpouring and ingathering of souls. We began having campus-awakening intercession before classes. At first I had to drag students there, and they would often fall asleep on me. Then suddenly, God's Spirit began to move in our prayer time, and more students started coming to pray. There are very few things that spiritually compare to being a part of a group of committed Christians calling out to God for souls and an awakening.

We lose the endorsement of God by leaning on our efforts alone, but when we rely on Him, He will endorse us just as He endorsed His Son:

> *Men of Israel, hear these words: Jesus of Nazareth, a Man endorsed by God to you by miracles, wonders, and signs which God did through Him in your midst, as you yourselves also know* (Acts 2:22).

We desperately need that supernatural backing to return to our basic Christian lifestyle. The depth of prayer required to trigger an outpouring is on a different clock than the internal clock of your typical Christian who is affected by the "instant-ism" of modern culture.

Prayer precedes a global harvest, according to Zechariah 10:1: *"Ask the Lord for rain in the time of the latter rain. The Lord will make flashing clouds; He will give them showers of rain, grass in the field for everyone."* Your petition is connected to His releasing "showers of rain." Nothing you are doing is more important than expending your soul in this caliber of prayer.

Eternity will reveal that all outpourings of God's Spirit were in response to people pouring their hearts out to Him while seeking His face. In *Unlock Your Hidden Prayer Power*, Brother Andrew says:

> God's prophetic will, no matter how clearly set forth in the scripture, cannot happen until His conditions are met. Not everything goes according to the plan of God... God gave His only begotten Son, the most crucial aspect of His plan. Why, then, do not all subsequent events go according to God's plan? Because God is looking for intercessors for the world.[6]

Zechariah emphasizes that it is in the Father's heart to give the Latter Rain. James emphasizes that the motivation behind the latter rain is for the precious fruit of the earth, which will be the historically epic, end-time, worldwide harvest of souls:

> *Therefore be patient, brethren, until the coming of the Lord. See how the farmer waits for the precious fruit of the earth, waiting patiently for it until it receives the early and latter rain* (James 5:7).

If Pentecost was the early rain, imagine what God has in mind for the latter rain! Like Cornelius in Acts 10, whose prayer ascended as a monument before the Lord and was answered with the Gentile Pentecost, we must also give ourselves to prayer. Leonard Ravenhill said, "God does not answer prayer, He answers desperate prayer."[7] Might it be that we emphasize our programs and have not emphasized enough discipleship that produces revival prayer warriors?

In the early 1800s, Samuel Mills, a pastor's kid and student at Williams College in Massachusetts, began organizing prayer meetings for a move of God. One day in August of 1806, under dark thunderstorm clouds, the group met outside for prayer. The thunderstorm became so violent that they sought shelter in a large haystack. You've heard of "See You at the Pole"—this was "Can't Find You in the Haystack"! As they hid in the haystack, they continued to seek God in prayer.

During this strategic instant of prayer, not only did a natural outpouring manifest, but a spiritual outpouring was brewing as well. Samuel felt impressed to share that they should go to India to preach the Gospel. This became known as the "Haystack Revival," and it led to a mission's movement and harvest of massive fruit in the nations. Their revival also led to the Student Volunteer Movement, where tens of thousands of college students went to the ends of the earth. It is impossible to ever know the full extent of what you will set in motion when you start praying for a move of God.

What does it mean to seek God's face? It means that we must seek the knowledge of God and His ways. By developing intimacy, we come into fresh fire because of fresh impact. The history of revivals is filled with accounts of fervent prayer. In George Whitefield's time, during the 18th century, people would cry out to God all night, overwhelmed by the glory of God. Intercession was the catalyst for the great Moravian revival of 1727. They were so possessed by His presence that they felt pressed to pray 24/7 for over 100 years, which seriously impacted the globe. In 1859, over 100 prayer meetings began simultaneously in Ulster, Ireland, even in graveyards. In the Scottish isles of Lewis, a blacksmith cried out to God and an earthquake hit his house as wave after wave of divine power swept through the house. As this prayer meeting finished, everyone went outside and found people rocking in the presence of God all over the community. I believe that there is a cry for revival that God is releasing to people that makes them dissatisfied with anything less than an outpouring of the Spirit that shifts a nation to God.

Stage 5: *"...turn from their wicked ways...."* Turning from one's wicked ways is a call to return to a lifestyle of personal holiness. Revival will not come, let alone be sustained, without Christians committed to holiness. Your impact on your culture and your ability to speak into other people's lives will be severely blunted if you are not free from the spirit of the world. We are a generation that is savvy to fakes and hypocrites. You cannot be frozen in a fallen culture when God has chosen you to set that same culture free.

The world is watching and is desperate for people who believe it enough to live it. If your individual temple is polluted, then your ability to synchronize with Heaven is critically limited. Your ability to hear the voice of God and be led by His Spirit will suffer. The coming revival in our day will place a demand of personal and corporate preparation among God's people. The enemy wants to see potential emerging revivalists caught up in the intoxication of this age. You are going to be tempted on every side, but Heaven releases its holy weaponry to equip you to stand against all attacks.

Becoming a Terminator of Transgressions

You can have all the revival you can handle. God wants to pour His Spirit out on us in such *great measure* as to blow away our previous ideas of a move of God. God isn't clogging the pipe of a historic outpouring—we are! Frequently, it is unbelieving believers who hold back the river of God because they seriously lack alignment (with what the Father has on His mind) in their lives. Often, we are asking God to pour out His Spirit and change our geography without actively participating ourselves.

When my son Brandon was born, my wife and I prayed and asked God to give us a prophetic middle name for him. The Lord impressed upon us the name Josiah, which means "the Lord burns" or "fire of the Lord." Again, King Josiah saw one of the most insane revolutionary revivals ever! Josiah got God's attention by turning to the Lord in one of the darkest eras of the Old Testament. King Josiah's grandfather was Manasseh, who dragged Israel's Southern Kingdom into total debauchery by Xeroxing the wickedness of the godless nations around him. Manasseh led them into worship of idols like Molech (involving baby sacrifices) and Baal (involving sexual rites). After 55 years, his wicked son Amon took over and things got worse. Judah was reeling in a dark abyss of murder, immorality, idolatry, and witchcraft, and the jaded people had forgotten their God. (See Second Chronicles 33.) Then Josiah, a "burning one," became king at an early age:

> *Josiah was eight years old when he became king, and he reigned thirty-one years in Jerusalem. And he did what was right in the sight of the Lord, and walked in the ways of his father David; he did not turn aside to the right hand or to the left. For in the eighth year of his reign, while he was still young, he began to seek*

the God of his father David; and in the twelfth year he began to purge Judah and Jerusalem of the high places, the wooden images, the carved images, and the molded images (2 Chronicles 34:1-3).

While Josiah was still young, he sought after God. At 8 he became king, and at 16 he began to seek God and began to stage a reform. Similarly, Charles Spurgeon began preaching when he was only 16, and Gypsy Smith, who drew evangelistic crowds numbering in the hundreds of thousands throughout his life, was but 17 when he began. Josiah's young life was fueled along with the zeal of a prophet. Real prophets are challenged by mediocrity; they have an inner compulsion to fight darkness. Josiah caught such a vision of God's holiness that he could no longer tolerate wickedness and sought to recapture his nation for God.

The temple had been polluted and neglected while everybody was drunk on Baal. Josiah went on a one-man, false-altar-demolishing, wickedness-terminating rampage. In his battle to liberate his country, Josiah went to great lengths to purge his nation of darkness, even traveling to the mountains to remove the high places (demonic shrines in mountains). In a short time, all of Israel was outwardly cleansed of idolatrous practices that took almost two-thirds of a century to erect. After the smoke cleared and the dust settled, Josiah's nation returned to God:

Then the king stood by a pillar and made a covenant before the Lord, to follow the Lord and to keep His commandments and His testimonies and His statutes, with all his heart and all his soul, to perform the words of this covenant that were written in this book. And all the people took a stand for the covenant (2 Kings 23:3).

Turning from our wicked ways not only involves dealing ruthlessly with sin but also standing for truth. It is difficult to claim that we stand for truth if those around us don't even know that we are Christians with set-apart lives. Life is too short to be devoted to things with an expiration date. Like Josiah, let us spend our lives turning to God so that He would send down the rain of revival upon our nation.

Thinking Like a Puritan

Historic Christianity, the brand practiced by the early Christians and of the Reformation, was one of confident expectation. They expected Christianity to be explosive and to fill the earth. One thing is for sure: no one will work for the transformation of society if he or she first doesn't believe society can be transformed. Revival brings to the forefront the hope of a conquering Christianity that begins to smolder inside the hearts of emerging revivalists, which equips them to contend for historic breakthroughs.

The Puritans, alive during the 16th century and beyond, wanted a new Reformation movement. They believed that revivals would be the medium by which the Kingdom of God would advance in the world. They also recovered a belief that became known as revival Christianity. These guys were relentless when it came to a revival attitude and outlook. This dominated everything they thought about, talked about, and went about for centuries.

The Puritans were a catalytic critical mass of English Protestants that came from Luther's mighty Reformation. They felt that the Reformation should continue in the Church until they experienced the vintage realities of the Book of Acts leading to massive impact in the earth. They worked toward moral and societal reshaping. Their revival attitude had no place for despair-filled thinking that many modern Christians fill their minds with. We see evidence of modern Christians with despair-filled mentalities when they approach the endtimes with phrases like, "Beam me up, Lord," and "It's all over anyway, so what's the use." The Puritans didn't view the world as a wreck to be escaped from but as stolen property that rightfully must return to Jesus. Regarding the Puritans' impact, Ian Murray cited this:

Today men may wonder at the influence which changed the spiritual direction of England and Scotland so rapidly four hundred years ago, making them Bible-reading nations and witnesses to a creed so unflattering to human nature and hateful to human pride.[8]

Maybe the signs and wonders promised by Jesus could include more than physical healing and individual deliverance, but also cultural impact and national transformation. If we fall into end-times despair, we begin to feel that the only work left for God is judgment. Knowing history, however, proves that God does a work of redemption to crown His Son's sacrifice. Now I do believe that judgment plays into the equation and that there will be times of tribulation, but God is coming back for a victorious Bride, not a defeated one, at the wedding rehearsal. Genuine revival is a supernatural celebration of the supremacy of Jesus. Revival is a high-voltage burst of supernatural energy resulting in a mighty impact upon a community. Prayer movement leader Dave Bryant says, "Spiritual awakenings are when the Father wakes us up to see Christ's fullness in new ways, so that we move with Him in new ways for the fulfillment of His global purposes." This would sum up what the Puritans felt, highlighting the cooperation and alignment that occurs when we believe that God wants to change the nations through His Church.

Here's What Some of the Puritans Believed

John Wesley was one of the greatest revivalists of all time, and when he arrived in New Castle, England, in 1742, he wrote: "I was surprised; so much drunkenness, cursing (even from little children), do I never remember to have seen and heard before in so small a compass of time." He surprisingly went on to say, "Surely this place is ripe for Him who came not to call the righteous, but sinners to repentance."[9] The Great Awakening proved his assessment to be very accurate. Today we would say, "The world has gotten so bad; we just have to endure these tough times." The problem with that thinking is that it doesn't get you out of the bed in the morning to contend for revival and mass salvation like the Puritans did.

David Livingstone, who gave his life to open up Africa for the Gospel, believed for revival like Wesley did. After preaching to a tribe and feeling that it was a good meeting, Livingstone saw the Chief go back to his hut to get intoxicated. He could have been discouraged that his ministry had such little immediate fruit, but instead journaled:

> …but time must be given to allow the truth to sink into the dark mind and produce its effect. The earth shall be filled with the knowledge of the glory of the Lord—that is enough. We can afford to work in faith, for Omnipotence is pledged to fulfill the promise.

Another journal entry records:

> …a quiet audience today. The seed being sown, the least of all seeds now, but it will grow a mighty tree. It is as it were a small stone cut out of a mountain, but it will fill the whole earth.

Finally Livingstone wrote:

> [Missionarie's] great idea of converting the world to Christ is no [myth]; it is divine. Christianity will triumph. It is equal to all it has to perform.[10]

Today millions are being saved in Africa in an unprecedented outpouring, and I believe that Livingstone saw this from a distance. The Puritans had an attitude that banked on the supremacy of the Gospel and prophetic passages that distinguished them as a culture of hope and holy anticipation. The attitude of revivalists is seen in how they speak with a conviction that righteousness will prevail.

Finally Charles Spurgeon, considered one of the last of the Puritans, preached a sermon entitled "The Triumph of Christianity" from Psalm 22:27. In this sermon Spurgeon attacks the idea that we are not to hope for a glorious future on Earth, brought about by those who "foretell that we are nearing the period of decay, when something better will supplant the Gospel."[11]

Many believe that the world will get much worse before Christ returns, and unknowingly agree with the decline of spirituality, because many passages of Scripture detail that there will be wars, natural disasters, and social unrest at the end of this age. Although it is true that there will be an increase of these events, it is equally true that God is equipping us to be the salt of the earth (preservers) and co-laboring with us so that the kingdoms of this world will become the Kingdoms of our Christ (see Rev. 11:15). Let me further drive this point home by three passages that I'm gripped by that form my attitude for Gospel impact and revival:

> *For the earth will be filled with the knowledge of the glory of the Lord, as the waters cover the sea* (Habakkuk 2:14).

> *And this gospel of the kingdom will be preached in all the world as a witness to all the nations, and then the end will come* (Matthew 24:14).

> *After these things, I looked and behold, a great multitude which no one could number, of all nations, tribes, peoples, and tongues, standing before the throne and before the Lamb, clothed with white robes, with palm branches in their hands* (Revelation 7:9).

Imagine an aggregate, incomputable total of people John saw in a vision revealed in the prophecy of Patmos (the island where John was given Revelation). Remember on Earth, John saw few believers. But at the end of the day, there will be no closed nations, no remote tribes without witness. So you can bank on things massively changing. Regions closed to the Gospel or hardened to Jesus are about to open up, and people are coming into the Kingdom in gigantic proportions. Remember Jesus said that the fulfillment of His supernatural declaration of the Kingdom would precede His return. When these passages are digested properly, they remind us how much it is already in the Father's heart to bring about a tangible atmosphere of His presence coupled with a demonstrative power and a matchless message. When these two components are combined, they will have a power and encounter dimension to them that will have more influence than any of us can imagine. It is simply a Revival of all revivals, resulting in an innumerable altar call response (massive harvest). You see, God is way ahead of us…go ahead and pull the rip cord!

5

The Combination Code
of a Divine Moment

All moments in history are not equal; some are *epic* in their significance. In these divine moments, God sovereignly reveals Himself and His purposes, releasing an invitation to rewrite corporate or personal history. When willing vessels have a yes in their hearts, they can become the "hinge of history" on which a new door opens to a new divine possibility.

Leonard Ravenhill is credited with saying, "Prophets are God's emergency men for crisis hours." I believe that right now Heaven is positioning the greatest preachers in history. This is truly a fullness-of-time juncture. Matthew Backholer, author of *Understanding Revival*, defines fullness of time as: "a series of synchronized events coming together as one which unlocks and releases all that God has for that particular situation."[1] You might say that there are combination codes to unlock divine moments.

I can remember my locker was underneath an upper-classman's locker during my freshman year of high school. I always wanted to rush through my 38 to the right, 3 to the left, 19 to the right combination to quickly pop open my locker. Sometimes, I got freshman brain freeze, when people were standing over me, and I forgot my combination code. It was so embarrassing when this upper-classman and his girlfriend noticed the forgetful freshman. Similarly, I think that believers can feel the pressure of darkness crowding over our efforts and forget the combination code to unlock our divine moment.

Revival is for the wayward who have become numb of heart, spiritually fatigued, and dropped out of the race. Revival is also needed to remove selfish agendas and self-satisfaction. When a nation is filled with churches that have turned inward, there is a need to spiritually resuscitate them so they can become a thunderbolt of revival and deliverance. There is a process to becoming God's pipeline. Jonah had to go through an alignment process in his heart and actions before he could receive his assignment and bring revival to Nineveh. Divine moments don't open for us without our cooperation. Just as my combination lock had a sequence of three numbers, we need three things to unlock these *kairos* times: 1) revelation, 2) relinquishing, and 3) risk-taking.

Each person, in every generation, has a choice to either wander aimlessly or to strategically live a meaningful life. But in order to carry God's revelation, we must take steps of obedience so that we can *become* His revelation. This is where relinquishing comes in. Jonah had to relinquish his very life—scholars believe that he sank to the bottom of the sea before being swallowed by the fish. Similarly, I believe the flash points of revivals we have observed have seemingly come when the Church looks to have sunk to new lows. Relinquishing looks scary, and definitely requires overriding control issues that we innately possess, but it always proves to be explosive. Hosea reminds us that relinquishing is the hinge point for the healing and reviving of a people:

Come, and let us return to the Lord; for He has torn, but He will heal us; He has stricken, but He will bind us up.

After two days He will revive us; on the third day He will raise us up, that we may live in His sight (Hosea 6:1-2).

God is serious about raising you up. Quite possibly, you may find yourself in a position of frustration. Frustration is often felt when your experiences aren't living up to your expectations. This might be the greatest argument that you weren't meant to live a status quo life. Something is getting ready to emerge out of your life. Get ready for a ride that will lead to your date with destiny and the impact you were meant to have. There's something of the nature of God that must come through us during this hour—an explosion of truth and righteousness without regard for consequences. That's where you reach the point of risk-taking, the final sequence that unlocks the combination code of a divine moment.

Henrietta, Hollywood, and the Latter Rain Revival

There may not have been a more "fullness-of-time" season in the modern era than in the year 1948. If there was ever a divine moment where a combination code was found, this was it.

Henrietta Mears believed that knowing Christ was the most energizing experience and that the Christian's life should reflect this enthusiasm. Her primary focus was on high school and college-age young adults. On June 27, 1947, Bill Bright and Billy Graham were in a service that Mears was speaking at. After Mears spoke, some of the young men, including Bill Bright, asked her for prayer. Baldwin and Benson, biographers of Mears, describe that divine moment this way:

> As they knelt they were overcome by a sense of helplessness and inadequacy. They prayed into the late hours of the night, confessing sin, asking God for guidance, and seeking the reality and power of the Holy Spirit. There was much weeping and crying out to the Lord. At times, no one prayed as God spoke to them. Then

the fire fell. They saw before them the college campuses of the world, teeming with unsaved students, who held in their hands the power to change the world. The college campuses—they were the key to world leadership, to world revival.[2]

Mears became a direct, crucial influence on Bill Bright (founder of Campus Crusade) and Billy Graham. This divine moment spawned many awakenings on college campuses across America. Bright founded Campus Crusade's first branch at UCLA. It now operates in 190 countries and produced the *Jesus* film, which has played for 4.2 billion people.

Another young man in this prayer meeting was Louis Evans Jr., son of a Presbyterian pastor in Hollywood. He shared his experiences with a young actress he was dating named Colleen Townsend, leading her to commit her life to the Lord. Other Hollywood celebrities were rocked by this move, including Roy Rogers, Dale Evans, and others. By 1949, some Hollywood stars met in Henrietta Mears's cabin to pray for direction on how to impact the film industry for Jesus. Eventually, her living room was filled with celebrities, many of whom bowed their knees to Jesus.

Mears was great friends with J. Edwin Orr, a world-renowned revivalist. Orr also spoke to the stars and became the chaplain for the Hollywood Christian Group. This group also began to attract industry professionals behind the cameras and in production. The size required a move to the Knickerbocker Hotel. Billy Graham benefitted from these production specialists when he began his first film crusades.

Billy Graham was the morning speaker and J. Edwin Orr spoke at night at one of the Forest Home College Conferences in 1949. Billy Graham was scheduled for a downtown L.A. crusade, but struggled over it. He prayed with J. Edwin Orr and went out into the woods to seek God all night. In the morning Billy Graham told Orr that God "had given him a vision that something unusual was going to happen down the mountain in Los Angeles."[3] As Graham received the revelation, relinquished his doubts, and took the risks, the rest was history. The crusade was a success, with Hollywood notables confessing Christ. The newspapers picked up the story, and Graham became a household name virtually overnight.

While the evangelical awakening with Graham, Bright, and others was taking off, a healing revival was erupting at the same time. Oral Roberts, William Branham, Gordon Lindsey (who later founded Christ for the Nations), and others associated with the Voice of Healing led this revival. T.L. Osborn attended meetings led by Branham, and he observed Branham ministering to the sick. Osborn saw God use Branham to deliver a deaf-mute girl of an evil spirit. Osborn later said that he seemed to hear a thousand voices speaking at once telling him that he could do the same, so he launched into ministry. Osborn's crusade in Uganda in 1957 is said to have laid the foundation for the full-Gospel revival in that country and to begin a great river of the Holy Spirit, which was destined to flow out over East Africa and beyond.

The Saskatchewan Visitation

Another significant development was the Latter Rain Movement, which took place at a Bible school in Saskatchewan, Canada.

In the latter part of the 1940s, there arose a deep hunger among Pentecostals who were unsettled over the diminishing frequency of the manifestation of the gifts. Their cry was for a fresh visitation of the Spirit of God. Many believers began to fast and pray, especially after reading *Atomic Power with God Through Fasting and Prayer* by Franklin Hall.

On February 11, 1940, 70 students gathered at Sharon Bible College and prophesied that God was opening a door before them into the gifts and supernatural ministries. The next day, as chapel continued, a word came that declared that the restoration of the prophetic ministry was beginning and called the whole school to consecration. Around springtime, the school held a conference and hungry people came from hundreds of miles. People spoke of the tangible glory of God as people got healed, filled with the Holy Spirit, and delivered from evil spirits. One pastor received the gift of healing and was being so used of God that he could no longer confine his ministry to his own church.

Many other testimonies followed of a revival of Pentecost and very similar phenomena breaking out in churches all over America, Canada, and other countries. In July, they held a camp meeting in North Battleford and thousands gathered from all over the world. Day after day, the Word was taught with signs following—all day people were out in the power of God. These revivalists had prayed that people would immediately be filled with the Spirit when hands were laid upon them as in the Book of Acts. Many sick people standing in long lines were healed by God as people laid hands on them. Carl Brumback, a historian of the Assemblies of God, said:

> Great emphasis was laid upon fasting and prayer, spiritual worship, and gifts of the Spirit. The result was a genuine move of God. Key assemblies became centers of this revival within the Pentecostal revival. A thrill of hope surged through thousands of hearts; a new outpouring of the Spirit was falling upon the dry and barren land.[4]

George and Ern Hawtin were brothers and leaders at Sharon Bible College, and they launched out and became very influential in the early spread of this movement. At an Edmonton meeting, they saw the deaf hear, the blind see, cancer healed, and people with other sicknesses made whole. Lost people were getting saved, and the outpouring was being reported in many places. People were out in the power, speaking in heavenly languages and prophesying. This Latter Rain Revival went from 1948 to 1952. This revival greatly impacted the modern prophetic movement today. This brought the restoration of the following:

- The gifts of the Spirit, including tongues, are received through the laying on of hands.

- God has restored all the offices of ministry to the Church, including apostles and prophets.

- Divine healing can be administered through the laying on of hands.

- Praise and worship will usher God into our presence.

- Women have a full and equal ministry role in the Church.

- Denominational lines are blurred, and the Church will unify in the last days.

The Mindset That Releases Manifestations

Much of what you are and will become is determined by your mentality. The early believers walked in supernatural boldness and recognized the value of Spirit-led risk. Risk is so crucial to an end-time awakening. Your greatest life assignment is encoded in your heart, and it takes risk to release it. What you do when you feel afraid will determine your destiny. Risk becomes a catalyst to release the untapped things within you. An authentic Christian lifestyle requires risk. If you don't take risks, then you will only do what you know you can do. Like Bill Bright, Billy Graham, and Henrietta Mears, when God gives you a revelation, you must come to a place of relinquishing and mix that with risk. If these great saints had stayed in their comfort zone, instead of taking a risk and entering the miracle zone, the movements they pioneered would have stayed grounded. Many times, the Holy Spirit will limit His power to as much as we're willing to risk through faith. Faith is taking a risk to follow God into the realm of the unseen, unknown, and dimly understood.

I see God raising up a generation of believers who will do mighty exploits and take new territory like David's mighty men in Second Samuel 23. David's mighty men are not so much a class of people as they are an embodiment of a much-needed mentality. Kingdom risk is required for a generation to witness what revival should look like. Satan wants to scare the Heaven out of you. He knows what's at stake in this crucial moment.

How did David's men become so epic and step into legendary exploits? We know many of these guys gathered to David at the cave of Adullam.

> *David therefore departed from there and escaped to the cave of Adullam. So when his brothers and all his father's house heard it, they went down there to him. And everyone who was in distress, everyone who was in debt, and everyone who was discontented gathered to him. So he became captain over them. And there were about four hundred men with him* (1 Samuel 22:1-2).

David's mighty men started off discontented, distressed, and in debt. Basically they came to him emotionally, mentally, and financially dysfunctional, but David imparted his mentality to them and it raised their vision.

The adversary of your soul will try to convince you that you are disqualified, but God is after dependence, not perfect track records. Many who have been used in revivals and movements were far from perfect. Martin Luther had a foul mouth and could verbally lay into his students pretty harshly. In fact, when Luther was asked how he came to faith, he shot back that it was while he was on the toilet. The man could be crude, yet God used him to launch the Protestant Reformation.

Charles Spurgeon, known as the "Prince of Preachers," started a charity organization that now works globally. In 1856, as Spurgeon was preaching at Surrey Hall for the first time, someone in the crowd yelled, "Fire!" The ensuing panic and stampede caused several fatalities. Spurgeon was emotionally devastated and battled depression. Yet, he eventually pastored the largest church of his day and was considered to be a forerunner of the mega-church.

Three Principles for Developing a Personal Culture of Risk

Before you can unleash exploits, you must unlearn your fears. Your inner atmosphere determines your outer environment. The longer you tolerate something, the longer it dictates your experience. Unless you step out and risk, you'll never know the anointing within you, let alone develop it. Emerging revivalists in the last days are going to have to move out in a whole new dimension. If you draw back when God is trying to draw you out, you will miss out on what God is attempting to draw to the surface. Safety apart from God is only a mirage. The ultimate safe place to be is in the will of the Father.

If you don't turn your adversity into ministry, then your pain remains your pain. Typically, if there is no adversity, there is no opportunity to do something historic. The Philistines were David's personal nemesis. Some may think that the Philistines were trying to stop the mighty men from fulfilling their destiny, but the Philistines were their destiny. Defeating the Philistines released rewards for David's men in their hour of history. Many of us, like Spurgeon, have had adversity, yet God wants to turn the soft spots of our adversity into a landing spot for His enabling grace. Overcoming your adversity will enable you to experience the Father, and it will empower and qualify you to stand during the world's most critical hour. Many times, moving into position by faith so that God can work through you, releases Him to break forth in outrageous ways.

Boldness in taking risks doesn't eliminate uncertainties; it embraces them! Unanswered dilemmas and unsolved mysteries are the seedbed for the supernatural. The combination code for a divine moment often requires one to step into a place called "looking foolish." Faith requires risk, and the nature of risk includes the potential to fail. This next revival will demand that you live a life of risk by investing your life in something larger than yourself. Believers will be called upon in the days to come to live on the edge and rise to the prompting of the Holy Spirit.

There's no way that Shammah (one of David's mighty men) didn't feel his heart beat faster as the Philistines charged toward him while his fellow soldiers retreated (see 2 Sam. 23:10-12). But then again, we don't know the other soldiers' names, just Shammah's. History is ready to record your name—just step out. You have the combination for your divine moment.

Moving From Domestication to Desperation

Many times in seasons preceding revival, people become more attuned to what is missing in their spiritual life. Believers can no longer tolerate the difference between what God has done and what we are currently living in. What once seemed to be a baby gap now appears to be a Grand Canyon, creating a significant, divine yearning for what's missing in our current experience. Desperation is one of the dominant heartbeats of all great revivalists; they *yearn* to see a true move of God. There's a hunger in the human heart to see God's power and glory. Everyone thirsts for this reality, but the real question is this: what well are you drinking from? Every revival was propelled by people who were so desperate to see the lost come to Christ that no price was too excessive.

In my book *Prophetic Evangelism,* I tell a story about a desperate man who came up to me as I was leaving a church office. This guy held a gun in his hand and threatened to kill me and then commit suicide if I couldn't give him a good reason to stop. After talking unsuccessfully with him for about an hour, I convinced him to come into a deli, hoping that this would buy some time. I had become desperate and was at the end of myself. I asked if I could bless the food I bought, and he impatiently allowed me to pray. As I prayed, I threw in, "God, I pray that you will help Rocky." Suddenly, he interrupted me. He said he felt a hand come upon him, and something was telling him to let me pray for him.[5] After leading him to the Lord and seeing him delivered, I was driving home talking to the Lord. I sensed the impression that desperation always brings God on the scene.

I was told about an incident, that happened not too long ago when a Ugandan revivalist was invited to speak to some American pastors on the subject of revival. He told them that their persecution brought desperation and their desperation brought revival. I believe that desperation cultivates revival in the womb of God's people. Desperation is not the move before the move; it *is* the move.

Out-of-the-Box Desperation

On only one occasion, Jesus declared that a certain act would have worldwide recognition wherever the Gospel of the Kingdom goes:

And being in Bethany at the house of Simon the leper, as He sat at the table, a woman came having an alabaster flask of very costly oil of spikenard. Then she broke the flask and poured it on His head. But there were some who were indignant among themselves, and said, "Why was this fragrant oil wasted? For it might have been sold for more than three hundred denarii and given to the poor." And they criticized her sharply. But Jesus said, "Let her alone. Why do you trouble her? She has done a good work for Me. For you have the poor with you always, and whenever you wish you may do them good; but Me you do not have always. She has done what she could. She has come beforehand to anoint My body for burial. Assuredly, I say to you, wherever this gospel is preached

in the whole world, what this woman has done will also
be told as a memorial to her" (Mark 14:3-9).

This woman walked into the midst of a religious atmosphere. Revival is the fresh recognition of Jesus in our midst. The presence of God in the midst of people has always been the catalyst for reformation. This woman had a choice—she could back off and allow the religious crowd to dominate, or she could side with desperation. She made history with her choice. Revivals bring a change of hands, from religious systems to a fresh revelation of who is in our midst.

There are three aspects to revival-triggering desperation. First, *desperation brings expression to the deep things within.* Desperation causes people to move beyond convenience and fleshly dignity into an intimate encounter with God. Recently, the Lord said to me, "You have become domesticated." I didn't understand or agree with that statement at first. But after some prayer, I looked up the term "domestication" and found it comes from the Latin word describing how wild plants and wild animals were turned into houseplants and house pets. The word means: "to make ordinary, to tame, to adapt to one's environment."

I then realized that I had lowered the trajectory of what I was aiming for because of the gifts and influence the Lord had given me. This happened so subtly over the years that I didn't pick up on it. Again, many people first come into the Kingdom with great vision, but disappointments, disillusionments, and other "disses" knock down their spiritual aim. Revival resets our spiritual vision so that we are aiming for the ultimate intention of Heaven in our generation. We may come to the cutting edge of what God is doing in a season, but if we don't progress, it's no longer a cutting edge, but a comfort zone. Revival comes to the Body of Christ to get our edge back and to put desperation in our spiritual nutrient system.

The woman in Mark 14 broke a box of ointment costing approximately a year's wages. The social customs of that day prohibited this lady from speaking in the presence of these men. Even though this woman was not allowed to express herself vocally, she went for the most extravagant expression she could think of. Her desperation would not allow her to walk away without tapping into the depths of her heart to express worship to the King. Desperation squarely focuses you on the beauty of Jesus. You grow in tenacious passion toward the Son of Man, Christ Jesus. In *Pursuit of the Holy*, Corey Russell says:

> We are cold in our affections, our sacrifices, and our devotion because we lack the true revelation of Christ. When Jesus is truly revealed to us, we are awakened to love—love that causes us to forsake all the fleeting pleasure of this temporal age and throw ourselves into eternal things, into the age to come.[6]

The second aspect of desperation is that *it makes us sensitive to grasp our divine moments*. The divine moment in which the woman poured out the costly ointment was critical in the Kingdom. Jesus was about to be crucified, and nobody around Him realized it. Many believed that Jesus would set up an earthly, political kingdom. I don't even think that she knew that she was engaging in a divine moment, but her desperation led her to tap into the moment more fully than anyone else. It was customary to anoint bodies for burial, especially kings' bodies. Desperate people become unconsciously prophetic and are led into history-altering acts at strategic times. They perceive things that domesticated people cannot.

I believe a generation is being raised up that has laid down their rights and shaken off mediocrity in pursuit of the One. They won't cave in to peer pressure. They aren't here to be popular or politically correct, but prophetic and biblically correct. They will emerge with the most phenomenal timing ever. Get ready!

The emerging revivalist will be enthralled enough to have a counter-flow of desperation to their domestication. God breathes on people and something comes out of them at a crucial point in time that seems to tip the scale.

Finally, the third aspect of desperation is that *it always has atmosphere-altering effects*. This woman changed the atmosphere when she broke the box to release the fragrance. She not only anointed Jesus, but the whole house, and everyone in the room left smelling good. But more than that, the release of her desperation and worship attracted the atmosphere-altering, history-making reality of Heaven. This is why the Lord declared that her act would forever be included in the Gospel.

Cornelius was another whose desperation attracted the atmosphere of Heaven. God told him that his desperation, which released a flash flood of intercession and sacrifice, erected a memorial before Heaven:

> *About the ninth hour of the day he saw clearly in a vision an angel of God coming in and saying to him, "Cornelius!" And when he observed him, he was afraid, and said, "What is it, lord?" So he said to him, "Your prayers and your alms have come up for a memorial before God"* (Acts 10:3-4).

This word for "memorial" here is the same word used in Mark 14:9 to describe the woman's fragrant offering. Desperation creates an irrefutable, conspicuous spiritual landmark that Heaven cannot resist. We must get to the place where we qualify as poor in spirit, for those who are poor in spirit receive the Kingdom of Heaven. When the Kingdom comes, what takes place in Heaven takes place on Earth. Cornelius and the woman, two "unknowns," became memorable by being spiritually hungry enough to get tenacious to a place of sacrifice and obedience. If you descend into despair, you will be forgotten, but if you ascend in desperation, you will be remembered.

6

Moved Upon to Embody a Movement

Movements have altered modern history because God moved in the individual lives of people to make a difference in the world around them.—Alvin Reid

Ideas that don't move people and inspire them to act have never changed individuals, let alone history. Movements are marked by a compelling vision for the future based on a strong set of convictions. Movements require a sacrifice where individuals put the vision ahead of their own agendas and convenience. Movements are also *culture-changing*, and depend on *culture-making* leaders to rise up. The world has boundaries defined by what the masses believe is possible and acceptable and what they believe is out of bounds. Revival forerunners are those who dare to push against those boundaries to determine how resistant these constraints are to change.

The Gospel of the Kingdom seeks to change people and renew culture. Christianity is a movement, not an institution, as many would love to define it. When speaking of revivals, you are describing an extreme movement that has the potential to see Heaven invade Earth in a radical way.

In every movement, whether sociological, political, or spiritual, somebody had to step out, or the movement would never have taken off. God wants to unveil your divine moment to step out, but He also wants to give you a vision for the movement beyond the moment. I've always felt that big people see the big picture—in spiritual hi-def, Kingdom, widescreen view. A conviction grows from this revelation of the big picture and becomes a driving force within forerunners. Next, a chain reaction follows where others are inspired and drawn in.

Think of how fads, trends, and cultural crazes catch on. At the beginning, someone has to look odd by putting herself out there long enough for others to catch on. I can remember when 501 straight-leg jeans, top-sider shoes, and alligator polos were very popular in the '80s. The first people who wore them looked like they were from *Happy Days* (the old television show based on the '50s). I remember thinking, "That is the oddest look on a guy." I was fresh from urban Oakland, and we had a whole different look. The first guys to rock that outfit on my campus stood out, to the point of generating comments. But within two semesters, that clothing choice had so caught on that I was sporting some Sperry's, 501s, and a pink (OK, salmon) alligator polo shirt.

Many movements take off because people see the big picture and leverage their influence to start something. You are in the Kingdom today because someone was willing to "wear Jesus" and look different enough to change your "taste." Those college kids didn't care if others talked or mocked; they felt cutting-edge and displayed the temperament of pioneers. That's why you must get beyond embarrassment. Passion takes you to the juncture on the other side of self-consciousness. No one can force you to be passionate for the Kingdom, but neither can anyone take away your passion.

Student Volunteer Movement and a Sleepless Night

Imagine being a 16-year-old, prize-winning debater at Cornell University and giving up your father's business to step into the Father's business. John R. Mott's life changed forever when J.K. Studd (that's his last name, and it fits), brother of C.T. Studd, came to speak a series of missionary messages in American colleges. On January 14, 1886, he spoke at Cornell. Mott arrived to hear Studd say, "Seek not great things for yourself. Seek them not. Seek first the kingdom of God."[1] That night, Mott couldn't sleep nor shake the phrase he had heard. Mott sought out Studd and had a talk that forever changed his life. Never underestimate one encounter with the Holy Spirit and what could be set in motion through your obedience to jump into what the Father is doing.

Later that summer, while representing Cornell at the first international Christian student conference held by evangelist D.L. Moody, Mott heard a speaker from Princeton give a missionary challenge. A hundred students signed the "Princeton Pledge," including John R. Mott. These guys started the Student Volunteer Movement (SVM), of which Mott was made chairman. The rallying cry of this movement was, "The evangelization of the world in this generation." They held a SVM conference in 1891 in Cleveland that was the largest student conference assembled to date. The SVM sought to enlist every Christian in the objective of evangelizing the world. They were highly successful, for in half a century more than 20,000 students reached the foreign mission field, an astonishing achievement. D.W. McWilliams said this at the movement's 25th anniversary services:

> I think it is no exaggeration to say that the influences that have gone out from these school grounds on which

we have gathered this afternoon in some respects have changed the history of the world...I do not think the history of the past 25 years can be written without putting in it something about the Student Volunteer Movement which originated here at Mount Hermon.[2]

John R. Mott went on to win a Nobel Peace Prize in 1946 for developing volunteer movements. He wrote about how to build Christian movements. I want to rephrase his points about starting movements.

Mott on Movements

Without the ultimate Prime Mover, your movement isn't budging. Jesus must be at the center of your life and the constitution of your movement. Movements have a dominant focus, and nobody inspires the human heart like the utter beauty of the Messiah. You must have a zeal for your Father's house that consumes you. We have had so much teaching over the last decade on purpose, yet I've never seen so many people walking around without a purpose. The primary issue is that it's not about you and me finding our own purpose, but discovering His purpose in Christ and fulfilling our assignment in that larger purpose. We were made alive and raised up by Jesus that He might show off His priceless grace. You and I become His workmanship, uniquely crafted and divinely designed for good works (movements), which God has made ready for us. Under the pressure of performance and mistaken assignments, we lose sight of our basic purpose to pursue intimacy with Jesus and love those around us.

When it comes to movements, the more impossible, the more appealing. John R. Mott said it is the impossible that brings out our own latent powers. You need to constantly bite off more than you can chew, get in over your head, and see impossibilities bow to Jesus. Mott said, "The heroic appeal makes possible the heroic response." Sometimes North American Christianity suffers in its appeal because it's not presented in a manner extreme enough to captivate a YouTube, adrenaline-junkie, X Games generation. Christianity in the Book of Acts was radical and fanatical. We don't need any more watered-down sacrifices, discount devotions, and especially no virtual-reality virtues. We need to lay our hand to the plow of His movement and not look back.

Successful movements require that you appear on the battlefield. The ultimate outcome of any movement is not achieved in a saltshaker, where Christians hang out. You and I must go mainstream with our movement. You weren't meant to hide in the closet; you are destined for campuses and coliseums. The believers in the upper room didn't stay there; they stepped out into the open air in Jerusalem and went to the uttermost parts of the earth (see Acts 2). Regarding the 1735 Northampton Revival, Jonathan Edwards wrote, "There was scarcely a single person in the town, either old or young that was left unconcerned about the great things of the eternal world."[3] This only happened because the movement left the building.

Movements that raise the bar, and blow the roof off, elevate the human spirit. Mott said, "Christ never hid His scars to win a disciple." We shouldn't be afraid to challenge a generation to sacrifice. All movements have a cause and a call to spread a message. Mott emphasized, "We should never be content with second best."[4] In other words, he didn't want humanism, violence, false religion, or darkness to win on his watch, and so he discipled all who would listen to him. This philosophy must affect whom we hang out with and allow to influence our lives. Choose your friends; choose your movement. Since I've known Christ, I've always sought to get people in my life who challenge me and are people of vision and conviction. Being around the fervent at heart has always kept me on fire. Look for those who are captivated by His presence and desperate to see God move in their generation.

Movements look to grow and enlarge priorities. The sum of Mott's work makes an impressive record: he wrote 16 books in his chosen field; crossed the Atlantic over 100 times and the Pacific 14 times, averaging 34 days on the ocean per year for 50 years; delivered thousands of speeches; chaired innumerable conferences. It's no wonder the man brought home the Nobel Prize. That takes focus, passion, and perseverance. Your daily devotional life must be a priority in your life if you are looking to grow. You must set aside time to get in His presence and learn to walk in it. A generation is coming forth that will do whatever they have to do to be spiritually ready to seize opportunities. One of the greatest challenges of sustaining a movement is the demand it makes on one's inner life. We must have character and be authentic, free from a double life. Once a movement gets underway, there's a temptation to be prematurely satisfied with something less than what the Father wants to give us. At this stage, God will often release a precious gift of holy dissatisfaction. This holy dissatisfaction creates a longing for things to be different. Without a passion for fullness, the enemy can cause the dust of complacency to settle in. Go out today and launch a Jesus movement, but let it begin in you!

The Jesus People Movement

The Jesus People Movement (JPM) broke out spontaneously on the West Coast of the United States in the late '60s and spread throughout North America and Europe. Many say the JPM commenced in 1967 with the opening of a small storefront mission called the Living Room in San Francisco's Haight-Ashbury district. Around the same time, Linda Meissner from Teen Challenge shared her prophetic vision for an army of teenagers marching for Jesus in Seattle. There was a staggering reaction of radical young converts and a formulation of Christian coffeehouses and communes all directed at winning a wayward generation.

The '60s were a decade of social, political, and spiritual experimentation and chaos. Phrases such as "post-Christian" and even the "death of God" were used to describe this time. In 1962, the Supreme Court began what David Barton called "an all-out and widespread war against religious principles." In Engel v. Vitale, verbal prayer in public schools was ruled unconstitutional.[5] In 1960, 100 years after the first condom, the first commercially produced birth control pill was made available, paving the way for the explosion of "free love." By the late '60s, church attendance was down, religious book sales slumped, and finances dropped off. John Lennon of the Beatles said, "Christianity will go; we're more popular than Jesus now."

But he couldn't have been more wrong. The next year, God released a revolutionary redemptive wind. Almost at the close of the decade, an awakening of faith occurred, largely impacting hippies, drug addicts, and young people. A generation felt uneasy over the political corruption, Vietnam, an economic recession, civil rights injustices, and stale religion. This generation had also been traumatized by JFK's assassination, the National Guard shooting of Kent State students, the assassination of Martin Luther King Jr., and much more. Professor of American history Erling Jorstad said, "By the late 1960s it seemed apparent that American religious and secular life was moving in directions which in earlier days had let it to revival."

The Jesus People Movement was a refuge from the counterculture of drugs, sex, violence, and spiritual experimentation. Many felt that this "hollow experimentation" called "freedom" had failed them miserably, so they became Jesus Freaks. These youth, who had been searching for some transcendent and experiential high, found their ultimate in Jesus Christ. As this movement began to gain steam, Christian music festivals, counterculture churches, underground Christian newspapers, and Jesus marches grew. Everywhere the revival flames burned. In Tennessee, an evangelistic festival planned for one weekend went on for 35 nights. One witness wrote, "I have never witnessed such a mighty outpouring of the Holy Spirit. The scene is unbelievable. I sit in the middle of a contemporary Pentecost." Estimates of those involved taken at the height of the media coverage in 1971 were upward of 3 million, spreading through 70 countries.

The original identifiable counterculture "Jesus Freak" was Ted Wise, who went from weed smoking to street witnessing in South San Francisco in late 1966. He and his wife set up the Living Room ministry on the corner of Haight-Ashbury. They were testifying and winning scores of hippies during the "Summer of Love" in 1967. The Wises wanted to return to Book-of-Acts, vintage Christianity. They witnessed to people and brought them back to the Living Room for food and discipleship. They established the first Christian commune, the House of Acts. In two years they had connected with literally thousands of young people.

Meanwhile, a counterculture evangelist, Arthur Blessitt, opened "His Place" nightclub, a ministry where teenagers could get some grub and the Gospel. Blessitt had regular toilet services, where new converts would flush away their drugs and bondages. He told youth to "drop a little Matthew, Mark, Luke and John," and get "naturally stoned on Jesus."[6] Once, Blessitt was witnessing to a young lady whose biker boyfriend didn't appreciate it and confronted Blessitt. The guy, named Buddha, had laryngitis and was a part of the "Jokers out of Hell" motorcycle club. Blessitt took him outside and prayed with him. Buddha got healed of laryngitis and prayed aloud to receive Jesus as Lord. Afterward, Buddha got off his knees and said, "Now, I'm really a joker out of hell, ain't I?"[7]

The term "Jesus People" was coined by Duane Pederson, who founded the *Hollywood Free Paper*, which at times reached nearly half a million copies in circulation. From 1969 through 1975, this paper served as a tangible voice and billboard for the JPM. Pederson was involved in street ministry on the tough boulevards of downtown Hollywood. He said everywhere he went he saw underground papers preaching sex and drugs and he knew something was missing. Within two days of Pederson handing out 10,000 copies of the *Paper*, his box was jammed with mail from street people wanting to know more about Jesus.

It was during this great movement that evangelist Mario Murillo became burdened for his generation. Dick Williams, a young teenage believer who pastored the Chi Alpha campus ministry at UC Berkeley, gave Mario a prophetic word. After God dealt with Mario concerning this word, Mario came to Berkeley to help Williams. Mario watched riots and protests for weeks and got a burden for his generation. In 1969, Murillo moved to L.A. and got on staff at Melodyland Church, which was a hot spot during the Charismatic Renewal. Dave Wilkerson, Winkie Pratney, Kathryn Kulman, and many others would come and minister there. There were altar calls when 1,000 people got saved at one time; the Jesus Movement was rising.

Dave Wilkerson gave Mario Murillo another prophetic word, and Mario moved back to Berkeley to help Williams again. They traveled to Chico State and joined hosting student leader Gaylord Enns, where they stepped into an outpouring. They held salvation meetings three times a day to accommodate the harvest. Later, Chico would host major Jesus Festivals where many thousands would come to hear musician Keith Green, Winkie Pratney, and Mario Murillo. Students came to Christ in droves!

In 1970, Mario rented a storefront on College Avenue in Berkeley during the flames of a student revolution. It was obvious that God was birthing a movement. Resurrection City was launched as an outreach ministry to Berkeley University students and soon attracted students from all over northern California. Radical campus protestors were becoming lions of revival, winning their peers to the Lord left and right. Resurrection City soon outgrew every campus venue, the Veteran's Hall, the Berkeley Theater, until it moved to the Oakland Auditorium. There were many thousands that were saved, and incredible miracles literally transformed people right before everyone's eyes. Blind eyes opened, the paralyzed walked, spines straightened, and mighty deliverances occurred. There was even a gal who had lost her womb in a brutal rape who got healed! Mario Murillo continued to see many come to Christ, including many who are in the ministry today.

Lonnie Frisbee was also strategic in the Jesus People Movement. Some time after he was radically delivered from drug addiction, Chuck Smith, founder of the Calvary Chapel movement, recruited Lonnie to help him reach the counterculture. At the time, Smith was pastoring a church of 100 people in Costa Mesa, California. Lonnie and his wife left the House of Acts commune in San Francisco to go help Smith. In one of the early Calvary Chapel services, Chuck's wife Kay Smith prophesied that God was going to "bless the whole coast of California with a mighty move, which will move across the U.S. and touch the nations of the world."[8]

Smith put the Frisbees in charge of a Costa Mesa rehab/ evangelism house called the House of Miracles, and within days it had 35 converts. Lonnie led the Wednesday night Bible study, which attracted thousands. Lonnie described himself as a "seeing prophet," while others called him the "Spiritual Pied Piper" of the hippie generation. Under Frisbee's ministry, his most visible convert was evangelist Greg Laurie, whom he mentored. Laurie went on to found Harvest Crusades, which has gathered together over 4 million people in stadiums around the world. It was said that while Lonnie was at Calvary Chapel, over 4,000 people were converted and more than 2,000 were baptized in the Pacific Ocean.

Later on, Frisbee helped launch the Vineyard movement with John Wimber. After speaking at Wimber's church, Frisbee invited everyone 25 and under to come forward. Witnesses said it looked like a battlefield as young people began to shake, fall to the ground, and speak in tongues. These youth were so filled with the Spirit that they began to lead friends to Christ, baptizing them in Jacuzzis and pools across Yorba Linda, California. This event is credited as birthing the Vineyard movement. Unfortunately, Frisbee admitted to immoral behavior and had to step down. He later died of AIDS, and Chuck Smith eulogized him as a Samson-like figure.

Jesus People had a strong belief in miracles, deliverance, and healing. They unashamedly gave themselves to evangelism. What they lacked in theological depth, they made up for in zeal for Jesus Christ and love of others. They strived for social justice and were passionate to walk just like Jesus did.

When *Time Magazine* placed "The Jesus Revolution" on its cover in June of 1971, they said the following:

> There are signs that the movement is something more lasting than a religious Woodstock. It shows considerable staying power; many who were in its faint beginnings in 1967 are still leading it. It has been powerful enough to divert many young people from serious drug addictions.[9]

No doubt the JPM had an enduring legacy that still impacts the Body of Christ at large. I believe that there will be a new Jesus People Movement that will impact a new generation.

Evidence of a Bona Fide Revival

How do we know when a genuine revival has come? Is it possible to identify when a move of God crosses a line of demarcation and transitions into full-blown revival? I believe that some outpourings don't develop into full-fledged revivals due to missing ingredients. Ernest Baker, author of *Revivals in the Bible*, says, "A revival may produce noise, but it does not consist of it. The real thing is a wholehearted Obedience."[10]

There are individual revivals, micro-revivals, and macro-revivals. Obviously, an individual revival is one that a solitary person experiences. This results in an increase of passion and longing for Jesus and prayer, a new desperation for God's glory, and a burning desire to bring others into relationship with Christ. People who are carrying this spirit of revival have an intense yearning to see the Word and the Spirit impact their world together. These individuals have spent such time in the presence of God that they have not only changed; they carry the voice of change.

A *micro-revival* is when a small group of people, such as a prayer group or school, is revived. By definition, a micro-revival is isolated, and if it spreads to a much larger sphere of impact, it moves into macro-revival status. The length of duration can be briefer in a micro-revival than in a macro. God gives micro-revivals so that they will spread, but they are given in a seed form that must be cultivated. In micro-revivals, God has broken barrenness off of His people so that they are expectant, ready to birth new Kingdom realities. A sacrificial lifestyle characterizes their walk and there is love one for another.

Macro-revivals are historically the revivals with the widest scope of influence. When revival comes, one of the earliest evidences is that the presence of God overwhelms people so that they are physically unable to stand as His glory is amplified. Remember the atmosphere that surrounded Saul of Tarsus in Acts 9—it knocked him down! Imagine that type of atmosphere, but on a larger scale where it impacts a group of people. If Saul was knocked off his horse, and went from persecuting Christians to writing half the New Testament, can you picture a region being hit by this dynamic? Imagine the glory that fell on the priests in Solomon's day as the atmosphere of Heaven came down and they could not stand to minister. What if the presence that was in the temple came and detonated over a campus, workplace, or the Strip in Las Vegas? That glory brings dramatic conversions as people get a revelation of an awesome God.

In the revival in Samaria, God anointed a deacon named Philip, whose voice was so spiritually amplified that a sorcery-bewitched generation *"with one accord heeded the things spoken by Philip"* (Acts 8:6). Likewise, right before Jesus came to Earth, John the Baptist was given a voice that resonated and captured the hearts of the multitudes.

Considering that John the Baptist wasn't doing miracles or handing out Starbucks Coffee or Krispy Kreme Donuts, it's amazing he gathered an entire region to hear his voice. Similarly, Charles Finney was once preaching in a village schoolhouse in New York, when people began to fall from their chairs and cry out for mercy. Finney says, "If I had a sword in each hand I could not have cut them down as fast as they fell. I was obliged to stop preaching."[11]

A revival must bring an understanding and an encounter. This makes for a full-effect witness that makes Heaven invading Earth a spiritual 3-D affair. Preaching is marked by a new power and a new urgency, whereby both Heaven and hell become more than concepts. Even the music and average testimony during a revival possesses an exceptional ability to cut to hearts of people.

Mas Fuego and Keys to a National Ignition

With every genuine outpouring of the Spirit comes the release of signs, wonders, and miracles that the Spirit uses to confirm the movement. In 1952, American evangelist Tommy Hicks received a "Macedonian vision" in prayer calling him to Argentina. He flew there and the Holy Spirit gave him the name "Perón." He later found out that Perón was the president of Argentina. Hicks requested permission to meet with him in order to secure a large stadium to have a salvation campaign. After President Perón witnessed a skeptical bodyguard get healed, Hicks gained permission to get an audience with him. The president, who suffered from an incurable skin disease, asked Hicks, "Can God heal me?" Hicks prayed with President Perón and he got miraculously healed. Hicks secured the stadium because the president was healed.

The capacity for Huracan Stadium in Buenos Aires was 180,000. It had never been filled before by any event. When Tommy Hicks held his event, the stadium was surrounded by huge traffic jams as thousands came from all over. The blind saw, the lame walked, the deaf heard, and ambulances that had brought sick people left empty. A three-year-old boy with braces on his legs, who had been unable to walk, was able to walk perfectly after prayer. The crowd went wild, and spontaneous healings broke out everywhere. The boy's doctor was so amazed that he fell on his knees saying, "I want this Christ. I want to be saved." Hicks preached for 52 days to a total of about 2 million, with over 20,000 converts. Signs, wonders, and miracles characterized both the Argentine revival then and the 20-year Argentine revival that began in 1985.

The later Argentine revival revealed that the supernatural is not limited to huge arenas. Manifestations of power will break out wherever God's vessels walk in the marketplace. You can't have a revival and contain it in a church building; it must have a significant impact on the surrounding community.

In revivals past, there have been some pretty dramatic alterations in the character and culture of a people. Ephesus was a great example of this:

> *This became known both to all Jews and Greeks dwelling in Ephesus; and fear fell on them all, and the name of the Lord Jesus was magnified. And many who had believed came confessing and telling their deeds. Also, many of those who had practiced magic brought their books together and burned them in the sight of all. And they counted up the value of them, and it totaled fifty thousand pieces of silver. So the word of the Lord grew mightily and prevailed* (Acts 19:17-20).

Paul actually witnessed people making public confession of what must have been serious immorality. They even torched the equivalent of 157 years of wages in occult paraphernalia in public view of the inhabitants of Ephesus. They actually demonstrated a holy indignation of their sins and showed a resolution never to return to the use of magic, and to turn instead to the counsel of the Word.

People who are touched by revival carry a unique DNA that won't let them settle for anything less than what they have experienced. When this massive revival boldness is released, these emerging revivalists will rise above their normal limits and tolerate no other allegiances. They are ready to die, if necessary, to embrace God's purpose. These burning ones long to overturn injustice and liberate people to experience God's liberty. The new breed of revivalists will look to mark their world with their faith and confront the powers of darkness with the powers of the age to come.

7

Forging A Revival Culture

A true revival means nothing less than a revolution, casting out the spirit of worldliness and selfishness and making God and His love triumph in the heart and life.—Andrew Murray

Have you ever failed miserably, run away from the scene of a floundering collapse, and then found yourself given a second chance to now reset history? Jonah did when the voice of the Lord came to him a second time. So did the disciples on the day of Pentecost—Peter, who had denied Jesus three times in front of a girl, made a proclamation that put a bull's-eye on his back. From this incident came the legacy of first-century believers winning multiple thousands to Christ. Regions were set on fire and turned upside down by ordinary men who stepped into Heaven's phone booth and came out with an "S" on their chest. Pentecost became the prototype for the revival cry and a blueprint for saturating the surrounding culture with the Kingdom.

Those who must win the world cannot be afraid to come in conflict with it. Any emerging revivalist who is a sign to his or her generation must be ready to outlast the opposition. He or she must have thick skin and a tender heart, for darkness will inevitably pull the trump card of adversity and misunderstanding.

When Jesus described John the Baptist, He was giving the characteristics of a forerunner generation that goes before a God move. Jesus asked, *"What did you go out into the wilderness to see? A reed shaken by the wind? A man clothed in soft garment?"* (Matt. 11:7). Jesus made the point that the Kingdom will be violently opposed, so we need a violent resolve to lay hold of it. One of the first challenges to come into a culture of revival is getting past the fear of man and the tool of intimidation.

Overcoming the Spirit of Anak

Before God delivers a region, He must first deliver His revivalists who are underground and sometimes overwhelmed by intimidation and despondency. Often when God is about to lead His children into new territory and release a long-awaited promise, the enemy conspires to get them to go back to old habits. Ian Malins addressed this in *Prepare the Way for Revival*:

> From a safe distance of several hundred years or several thousand miles, revival clearly looms exciting and wonderful…The strange thing about revivals, however, is that while they are so longed for in times of barrenness, they are often opposed and feared when they arrive. Why? Because revival is threatening. It disturbs the established order of things. And this brings conflict, fear, division and even opposition from other Christians.[1]

Revival brings heat in the spirit realm. This spiritual warfare weeds out the wannabes from the ones who change history. Revival brings a tornado that blows in the face of religious traditions and flesh. Many times a defining moment disguises itself as a crisis. A crisis is seen as a threatening situation from Earth's perspective, but from Heaven's perspective, it is an opportunity to discover something.

I grew up in a rough area of Oakland, California. I lived in an area where there were street gangs, drug dealers, and bullies. My mom and grandmother raised me. This may have contributed to my not learning how to fight well early in my life and developing a philosophy of avoiding conflict at all cost.

I had a bully cousin who lived with us, and he routinely used me as a punching bag. It's one thing to go to school with a bully; at least you can run home. When I did that, my bully would follow me home and continue the butt-whoopin.' One day, a bigger kid named Samuel, the fiercest kid in the neighborhood, got into a fight in front of our apartment and beat up my cousin Marty so bad that I just froze. I don't know if I would have helped him if I could. After being traumatized by witnessing Marty's beat down, I did some inner-city algebra. If Samuel could beat up Marty, and Marty could beat me up, I didn't need to fight Samuel.

One day, my best friend Anthony and I were taking a stroll through the hood. We turned a corner, and there was Samuel. He was enraged and punched me hard in the chest. After I flew back, he threatened me with, "If you know what's good for you, stay down." He then proceeded to beat up my best friend right in front of my eyes.

This was a defining moment—either I would sit back and do nothing to stop this beat down, or strike a blow to interrupt the thrashing. Either choice would define me from that time on. In that moment, I recognized that my philosophy of avoiding conflict wasn't working. I felt the most intense inner battle against the intimidation and inner picture of weakness that I had walked under for so long. But something happened. I suddenly felt like I couldn't live with myself if I didn't strike a blow to help my friend. So I balled up my fist and swung as hard as I could. I knocked Samuel out. He certainly didn't see it coming. I picked up my friend and got him out of there. I was never the same. I had conquered two foes that day—one mental and one physical. When you look over the darkness beating down your generation, you're standing in an eerily similar dilemma—to strike a blow for God or to be forced to watched anti-revival forces in destructive action.

In Numbers 13, the Israelites were standing at the edge of the Promised Land staring at its fruit, only to back down because of the Anakim (the descendants of Anak):

> *And they gave the children of Israel a bad report of the land which they had spied out, saying, "The land through which we have gone as spies is a land that devours its inhabitants, and all the people whom we saw in it are men of great stature. There we saw the giants (the descendants of Anak came from the giants); and we were like grasshoppers in our own sight, and so we were in their sight"* (Numbers 13:32-33).

The Anakim were incredibly huge people that would have made Shaq look dwarfed. The spirit of Anak neutralizes your warfare by causing you to lose proper perspective and to settle for less. We lapse into business-as-usual mode instead of breakthrough mode. We fall into a survival mindset instead of a revival mindset. Once the Anak spirit has taken root in your life, you'll start to lose your sense of purpose. The Promised Land represented the fullness of what the Lord had for Israel and an inheritance for future generations. What kind of territory has God told you to take in this season? Revivalists throughout the ages became Heaven's heroes because they overcame this spirit of intimidation. In front of every would-be revivalist are territories to be taken and an army of Anakim to be defeated. We must defeat the Anakim in warfare so that we can see community transformation.

Like my dilemma with Samuel, you can choose to stay intimidated, bow to your circumstances, and embrace an anemic, knockoff version of Christianity. Or you can emerge as God's revivalist on your campus or workplace. I believe you must contend for the revival designated for you.

The simplest scheme to upset the giants and defiants of your promise is the Law of the First Step. Sometimes God waits to act until you step out in faith to cooperate. The Law of the First Step begins when a person refuses to be downgraded from a truth. For Peter, this happened when he went public in the open square of Jerusalem as a burning prophet of new wine. Peter and the disciples were a sign to their generation, but only after they took the first step to overcome the spirit of Anak.

Overcoming the Spirit of Ahab

In studying revivals, I have found that it is essential to confront the oppressive spirit of the age so that an awakening can have its rightful impact. Too many Christians are question marks when they need to be exclamation marks.

Elijah dealt with this problem during his ministry:

And it came to pass after many days that the word of the Lord came to Elijah, in the third year, saying, "Go, present yourself to Ahab, and I will send rain on the earth." So Elijah went to present himself to Ahab; and there was a severe famine in Samaria. And Ahab had called Obadiah, who was in charge of his house. (Now Obadiah feared the Lord greatly. For so it was, while Jezebel massacred the prophets of the Lord, that Obadiah had taken one hundred prophets and hidden them, fifty to a cave, and had fed them with bread and water) (1 Kings 18:1-4).

I think this is going to be the saddest, darkest, most embarrassing piece of heavenly YouTube that can ever be replayed. The prophets were hiding in caves. Having the mouthpieces of God caved in at such a crucial time was horrible timing. For over

50 years, Israel had departed from the faith. Wicked King Ahab married Jezebel, creating an awful mix of idolatry, perversion, witchcraft, and a closed spiritual atmosphere to Yahweh. Baal was worshiped and the Temple in Jerusalem was deserted. Finally, orders were given to systematically overthrow the altars of God everywhere.

In verse one, God gives us the answer to the spirit of Ahab and a key to revival. God told Elijah to "go present yourself to Ahab," with the promised result that He would make it rain. It was as if God was saying, "If I can get you to move from the background to the forefront, I will move from the invisible to the visible." Too many potential revivalists are looking for safe places while God is looking for forerunners who are willing to go into dangerous places.

While other prophets were peering out of their caves, one prophet stepped forth and set in motion a chain reaction to eliminate Baal. Ahab represents the ungodly systems that put people in bondage. Like Elijah, spiritual awakeners of past reformations have been called to confront the ungodly systems holding generations in bondage.

The Human Smart Bomb for Reformation

The Word of God says that the spirit of Elijah would come again—and it did in the 15th century. When revival came to Florence, Italy, in 1496, the human smart bomb (one guided by the latest technology) of God was a monk named Girolamo Savonarola. As a youth, Savonarola would walk and weep over the sins, injustices, and oppressions of his people. For hours he would seek God's face for a spiritual awakening that would answer the crises of his day.

The immorality of the people and the corruption of the priesthood plunged the Church into a most degraded condition.

Initially, Savonarola didn't fare too well in the ministry, and people left his parish to attend elsewhere. Up to this time, Savonarola had not displayed any sign of the prophetic gifts. While waiting before God, he received a vision where the Lord told him to proclaim future calamities of the Church. Empowered with a new impartation, he now captivated his hearers. Revival started breaking out as he thundered against oppression and the sins of their society.

Find His Vision, Find Your Voice

People began to sob openly, and many walked the streets speechless while the Holy Spirit dealt with them. Savonarola challenged the people to burn accursed images and literature according to Acts 19:19. People destroyed thousands of pagan books, filthy pictures, lewd literature—it was called the *Bonfire of the Vanities*. Hymns rang out in the streets, and many followed Savonarola into ministry. He organized the youth into a sacred army that charged others with a standard for a holy life. Dens of prostitution shut down and theaters with perverse shows went "off Broadway." Gambling spots, as well as the racetrack, closed and Florence became a place where Heaven came to Earth.

Savonarola prophesied that the corrupt city ruler, the pope, and the king of Naples would all die within 12 months, and it happened. After receiving a heavenly download about an invasion from France, Savonarola went out to meet the French armies, faced them, and on two occasions turned them away. Meanwhile, Savonarola continued to denounce the abuses of the Church.

The corrupt priests were outraged at Savonarola. They incited a mob against him, broke into the sanctuary, and captured him. Savonarola was pressed to confess heresy before the people on pain of torture. His hands were tied and he was dropped from a great height so that his shoulders ripped out of their joints. But Savonarola would not back down from the truth. This spirit of

Ahab could not intimidate or cause this radical revivalist to cave in. They put burning coals to his feet multiple times and he would just kneel and ask God to forgive them.

Finally, Savonarola was slated for execution and was brought out before a crowd of thousands. They all quieted at Savonarola's last utterance: "Should I not die willingly for Him who suffered so much for me?" Savonarola didn't fear armies, rulers, or demons. During this revival in Italy, a young boy who lived in Germany would be greatly influenced by the life and death of Savonarola. That boy's name was Martin Luther.

Elijah Revisited

Ahab tried to pin the shame of a national crisis on Elijah. Elijah rightfully spoke up and decreed that Ahab and his house were at fault. This new breed of emerging revivalists must not allow political correctness to plant seeds of self-doubt and dump shame upon them.

In his book, *Sowing Seeds for Revival,* Martin Scott speaks of sins that affect the land. He mentions idolatry, sexual immorality, bloodshed, and broken covenants. All four of these tremendously affected the land under Ahab.

Elijah called the children of Israel together to put an ultimatum before them that should have been a no-brainer:

And Elijah came to all the people, and said, "How long will you falter between two opinions? If the Lord is God, follow Him; but if Baal, follow him." But the people answered him not a word (1 Kings 18:21).

On one side you have the Almighty Creator of the universe. On the other side you have a stiff figurine which represented Baal. Yet, Scripture says no one acknowledged this venerated prophet of God. You might say Elijah's first attempt at an awakening failed— it failed miserably.

All revivals have a three-part harmony: *First, darkness devastates.* It seems that right before a revivalist emerges and revival ignites, all H-E-L-L breaks out. This is where it seems like the Church has had her lights knocked out, but it only requires one spark of glory to alter that. *Second, dread champions detonate.* God so anoints His emerging vessels that it puts fear in the enemy's camp. Satan's worst nightmare is a righteous reformer who lives what he or she believes. *Third, dunamis demonstrates. Dunamis* is the Greek word used for explosive, miracle-working power. At this stage, God releases the supernatural as a heavenly endorsement of the bold steps of His burning ones.

After the jaded Israelites didn't respond, Elijah decided that it was time to unleash the outrageous DNA of God and not let the false prophetic voices go unchallenged. Mout Carmel, once a home to the altar of God, was now seemingly Baal's domain. Yet, Elijah essentially said, "Let's put it to the test. Whoever's God can answer by fire is the real sovereign in the land." All impostors would pay with their heads rolling. After the false god Baal (whose specialty was fire) failed to produce a spark, God sent a shekinah blowtorch that lit a water-drenched sacrifice.

Fire captured the spiritual atmosphere, and after the execution of 850 false prophets, Elijah decreed a rain of God's presence over a wicked nation. Get ready; the rain of God is almost here. I can see a cloud the size of a man's hand (see 1 Kings 18:44).

You have the same nature as Elijah. There's nothing wrong in asking for the spirit of Elijah, but you already have what it takes to make it rain:

> *Elijah was a **man with a nature like ours**, and he prayed earnestly that it would not rain; and it did not rain on the land for three years and six months. And he prayed again, and the heaven gave rain, and the earth produced its fruit* (James 5:17-18).

What Revival Produces

Supernatural presence will be a featured dynamic in the evangelism of the future, especially as revival is unleashed. When God's presence manifests outside the Church the way that He does at the altars inside, then you are having church wherever you go. Revival, however, results in God's presence manifesting with a greater intensity, and in a larger sphere, than at some of our best altar services.

It was said of Charles Finney that when he "opened his mouth, he was aiming a gun."[2] He saw over half a million people brought into the Kingdom through his ministry.

A woman sharply opposed the revival of Finney. She was strong-willed and very influential in the city. One night Finney spoke and then stayed after the service:

> [A man] came hurriedly to us as we were going out, and said "There is a lady in yonder pew that cannot get out; she is helpless. Will you not come and see her?" We returned and lo, down in the pew was this lady of whom I have spoken, perfectly overwhelmed with conviction… she found herself unable to stand and sunk down upon the floor."[3]

This was the same lady that caused trouble for Finney. The presence of God had so blasted and pinned her with conviction that she fell down and couldn't get up. Finney helped her up and led her to Christ.

Arthur Wallis says, "The spirit of revival is the consciousness of God."[4] It is also pretty evident that in revivals the awareness of the spiritual realm is heightened. This makes way for people responding to the unseen in ways that may seem dramatic. In revival, God's presence begins to overshadow individuals and saturate communities. When God shows up, resistance goes down:

The mountains melt like wax at the presence of the Lord, at the presence of the Lord of the whole earth. The heavens declare His righteousness, and all the peoples see His glory (Psalm 97:5-6).

When God comes in mighty power and sovereignty, He doesn't tolerate opposition to what He is doing. When people witness opposition decreasing, this impacts others, and other conversions follow in a domino effect.

A Love-Struck Teenager

In revivals, the person of Christ becomes center stage accompanied by a longing to be with Him and to shift all priorities to accommodate Him. I believe that so much of this generation's ADD is due to the fact that the activities and personalities of this lower world were never meant to keep us. We were created for fascination, to be awestruck by His ways. In moves of God, people are brought into the superior pleasures that come from feasting on the beauty of Christ.

The Welsh Revival of 1904 might be considered one of the most impacting revivals since Pentecost. Many know of the revivalist Evan Roberts who was associated with the awakening along with other great communicators. But it was none of these speakers, or committee programs, that lit the fuse. The fuse was lit in a weekly youth group meeting in New Quay, Cardigan, Wales, on February 14, 1904. Pastor Joseph Jenkins asked: "What does Jesus mean to you?" Fourteen-year-old Florrie Evan stood up in a meeting and cried out, "I love Jesus with all my heart."[5] Her heartfelt profession was like a Holy Spirit lightning strike in the congregation and the whole meeting caught fire.

Person after person arose and made full surrender to Christ. A visiting evangelist tried to close the worship service, but it "went on beyond human control." The news of the service spread throughout the area as young people testified in other churches. Those words became the first drops of an international divine downpour as fire quickly spread to young people in the Cardiganshire area. For Florrie, little did she know that her fiery heart and zeal for Jesus could thaw nations in a massive revival. When the lost see a supernatural love-struck look upon us, they are drawn to Jesus as if by divine magnetism.

Elevating Faith to Vintage Christianity

Prior to a revival starting, unbelief and immorality generally become prevalent in and out of the Church. This was definitely the case during the period before Martin Luther served notice to a corrupt clergy that launched the Protestant Reformation. Luther began to study Scripture and was captivated by "justification by faith." It was that revelation that served as a catalyst causing him to become a revolutionary. This launched a series of reforms within the Church that helped get Christianity back to what it ought to look like.

Luther had many opponents. One in particular, John Eck, was a genius who held a position at the University of Innsbruck. He rebutted Luther's 95 Theses and called Luther a despiser of the pope. Eck challenged Luther to a debate and Luther accepted. It lasted 18 days. The judges, who were somewhat crooked and leaned toward the corrupt pope, backed their boy Eck and declared him the winner. But like Rocky against Clubber Lang, Luther dramatically gained influence in Germany. These debates catapulted Luther into the spotlight in other countries until he became an international figure. When you stand for truth, even what looks like a setback will be your setup, if you step out.

There are a number of churches today that aren't looking or contending for what is revealed as the New Testament Church. James A. Stewart wrote:

> Coldness, deadness and backsliding are abnormal and the
> Church will never become normal until she sees revival.

The glorious splendor of the Church which shines out as a result of revival is the true standard our Lord has set up in the New Testament and this is what He expects among His redeemed ones at all times.[6]

The Word of God becomes so valuable to God's people during revival because it contains the revelation of authentic Christianity. It becomes their food, the air they breathe, and their delight. To preach revival is to return to the Word. In fact, when the Word and the Spirit consume people in ways that entertainment never can, this is proof that revival has come. Leonard Ravenhill wrote:

> When the Church gets a divorce from worldliness, when we recognize that the Bible written yesterday is also for today and for tomorrow, and that it alone has the formula for revival, we shall at least have started on the road to the reformation of the church, which must precede the true spiritual awakening which alone can save our generation.[7]

Paul wrote to the Thessalonians, asking them to pray *"that the word of the Lord may run swiftly and be glorified, just as it is with you"* (2 Thess. 3:1). His prayer is answered when revivals occur and the Gospel accelerates, overtaking regions like it had back in the day.

Go Forth and Grab the Harvest

Right before the 19th century, China was oppressed by other nations. This led to the Boxer Rebellion, where an uprising took place in response to imperialism. A blood bath followed in which, among others, a hundred or more missionaries were martyred along with thousands of their Chinese converts.

One missionary, Jonathan Goforth, narrowly escaped and went into a period of retirement to recover from the exhaustion of the persecution. He returned to China in 1901 and was dissatisfied with the spiritual harvest of his labors. He received a few written reports about the Welsh Revival of 1904 and a little booklet containing Finney's lectures on revival. Two things gripped the now desperate Goforth: 1) He realized that revival was not a thing of the past, and 2) that any group of believers could have revival if they would fulfill the necessary requirements.

Goforth was preaching at a great idolatrous fair in Hsunhsien and he saw Heaven break loose. Goforth said:

> It was at this fair I began to see evidence of the first stirrings in the people's heart of the great power. Convictions seemed to be written on every face. Finally, when I called for decisions, the whole audience stood up as one man crying, we want to follow this Jesus who died for us![8]

As these people began to pray, they broke down weeping. One Chinese evangelist who saw this said, "For almost twenty years we…had longed in vain to see a tear of penitence roll down a Chinese cheek."[9] This was the start of revival. At every place where Goforth preached, he saw men coming forward seeking salvation. Wesley Duewel wrote, "Noted witches and their whole families were converted. Hopeless opium addicts were saved and became powerful witnesses for Christ."[10] Then in 1907, Goforth went to Korea for three weeks and souls came to Christ left and right.

Later, Goforth broke open the spiritually cold Manchuria and saw powerful evangelism spread out. Thousands were converted and baptized. Demons were cast out, sicknesses healed, and addictions broken. Goforth stated:

> We wish to state most emphatically as our conviction that God's revival may be had when we will and where we will….We may be sure that, where there is a lack of the fullness of God, it is ever due to man's lack of faith and obedience. If God the Holy Spirit is not glorifying Jesus

Christ in the world today, as at Pentecost, it is we who are to blame.[11]

Goforth was simply desperate for a move of God and yielded to the Holy Spirit.

The Year of Grace—Ulster Revival, 1859

One of the most undeniable evidences of a genuine revival is the extreme spiritual makeover of any geography that becomes the flashpoint for such a blessing. In revivals, the spiritual atmosphere goes through a change of ownership. God seizes the environmental controls from darkness via His redeemed emerging revivalists.

In Coleraine, Ireland, God moved in such an off-the-charts way that an inscription was written in the town hall, "The Year of Grace, 1859." The Ulster Revival is one of the most dramatic examples in the history of Christianity of faith being so compellingly revived. The atmosphere in congregations was cold, prayerless, and worldly, but that would soon change. A layman named William Moore began preaching in Coleraine, Ulster, Ireland. His desire was to capture the hearts of the upcoming generation with the epic truths of Scripture. News of the Businessmen's Revival in America made it over to Ulster. Suddenly, these testimonies of revival became the catalyst that caused Ulster to tangibly thirst for a similar outpouring in Ireland.

In the Coleraine, Ulster, revival, a young boy was troubled while sitting in class. The teacher advised the boy to go home. An older boy who was a Christian followed him out and led the younger boy to Christ. The young guy turned around and went back to school wanting to testify. The teacher asked him why he had returned. The boy responded, "I am so happy. I have the Lord Jesus in my heart!" These words had spiritual nitroglycerin on them, because boy after boy slipped out of class. After a while, the teacher followed them and saw students on their knees sobbing. The girls' school was above, and soon all of them were outside crying out to Jesus. After a while, practically the entire school was enraptured in conviction. A united cry hit the streets till every available spot (even offices) was filled with sinners seeking God.

The revival spread rapidly like wildfire across Ulster. Hard-core unbelievers would break down on the streets weeping like babies. A young man fell on his knees in the middle of a crowded marketplace near Ballymena, crying, "God be merciful to me, a sinner!" People would go past people's homes and hear them praying, praising, or crying aloud for mercy. Everybody was calling on ministers and experienced believers. Every night, church services overflowed—thousands would just show up.

Prostitutes got saved and were thoroughly changed by the Spirit of God so that prostitution totally disappeared in Coleraine. Alcohol sales plummeted; bars were closing down.

Here's what Ian Paisley wrote in his book, *The Fifty-Nine Revival:*

> Very many of them received a marvelous fluency and power of prayer. A hatred of sin, a love for the Savior, a zeal for His cause and affection for one another, and an anxiety about perishing sinners, took possession of their hearts and literally ruled and governed their actions.[12]

People carried their Bibles everywhere they went; they would even stop on the road and read God's Word. Businessmen took vacations just to give themselves to prayer and the revival. In one place, about 2,000 went to a prayer meeting. One meeting lasted 42 straight nights, with thousands thronging the place.

The Fantastic Four of Fervent Flame

No super-renowned name is associated with the Ulster Revival, just hungry, rank-and-file believers. There was a young businessman, James McQuilken, who got saved and then led his friend Jeremiah Meneely to the Lord. They began to meet regularly to pray. Soon two others joined them, John Wallace and Robert Carlisle. These became God's raw material and Heaven's Fantastic Four of fervent travail.

They began to cry out for an awakening and they continued for several months. On New Year's Day 1858, the first convert was brought in. By the end of the year, 50 men were seeking God with them. Soon this holy revival culture they started covered the whole land in a vibrant manifestation of God. Meneely became the great evangelist of the revival. He preached with laser-like enthusiasm and carried the Gospel throughout the whole of Ireland, and across to Scotland and England. The Holy Ghost rocked the towns he visited with a spiritual earthquake that registered 8.0 on the revival Richter scale. People were abandoning entertainment to take to the streets, and they saw miracles. Grateful, loving, joyous converts began to multiply. The revival so gripped regions that even large buildings were not able to contain the multitudes that assembled.

So intense was the desperation for more of Him that it was recorded of one district, "Whole towns are awakened, all outdoor labor suspended, and the people in the crowds follow the minister from door to door to engage in prayer."[13] Often revival came to churches before the services even had a chance to begin. Many large evangelistic campaigns were held, where each service saw hundreds saved. They even had one of these evangelistic meetings on board the Kingston Holyhead steamer and saw everybody get saved, crew and all, except three members.

One particular attribute of this revival was the work of God among youth. They proved very open to the new move of the Holy Spirit. Some held their own services, with teenagers preaching the Gospel to hungry crowds of their friends. Female preachers were also used in this revival. Phoebe Palmer came to Coleraine and spoke at a number of meetings. Two female converts joined a group traveling around the region, preaching the Gospel to all who would listen. In August 1859, the *Morning Advertiser* said there were more conversions in the previous three months in Coleraine than there had been in the previous…perhaps 100 years.[14] Can you say "Flame On"?

8

Twenty Minutes to a Revival: Spontaneity and a Spiritual Awakening

Do not remember the former things, nor consider the things of old. Behold, I will do a new thing, now it shall spring forth; shall you not know it? I will even make a road in the wilderness and rivers in the desert (Isaiah 43:18-19).

Almighty God is not a once-upon-a-time Creator. He is the ultimate innovator, designer, originator, producer, and developer. He is still formulating new things in our day in order to bring His purpose to pass. He is still creating avenues and opportunities to bring redemption.

At the time of Isaiah's prophecy, Israel was in Babylonian captivity. It was not looking like they would fulfill their destiny; it looked like God had forgotten them. Yet, God said He would do even greater things and that their deliverance wouldn't look like anything in their past.

Think about it, the last thing you expect to see in the wilderness is a paved road. You really don't anticipate a river to just break out in the desert. Just before the sudden outburst of revival, people feel like their maps of reality severely malfunction. The well-worn paths lead to stalemates and impasses. A.W. Tozer once said, "When we come to the place where everything can be predicted and nobody expects anything unusual from God, we are in a rut."[1]

"Suddenlies" must be a consistent staple in the diet of God's people. Without these our faith becomes predictable and we get bored. We need the constant anticipation of a major move of God, the sense that Heaven could invade our world at any given moment. God has perfect timing and the Master of the out-of-nowhere, last-minute breakthrough. His sovereignty is seen in His timing of creating "roads" and "rivers." Just when you think there's no way, no strategy of redemption, or no strategic release of the Spirit that could possibly unfold, a "suddenly" appears. When looking at the timings of revivals throughout history, you begin to see that even the timing is part of the genius of Heaven's assault on darkness.

Just Another Chapel Service?

Imagine you're at a college that requires you to attend chapel. One morning you get up to make your 10:00 A.M. chapel service. Then, without any indication whatsoever, all Heaven breaks loose. Your 50-minute chapel goes 185 hours straight. You have continuing services for months as this spontaneously breaks out and is carried to other campuses and churches across the United States and even to other nations.

This happened at Asbury College in Wilmore, Kentucky. At a time when other students across America were burning down buildings and rioting on campuses, students at Asbury had something burning in their hearts and were about to see a holy eruption in a 1,500-seat auditorium.

The dean was supposed to speak but felt led to allow students to share testimonies. The dean opened by sharing, then student after student got up and testified and confessed their sins. As one shared, it was as if a lightning bolt hit another and he or she would get up, testify, and confess. When chapel was supposed to end, one of the professors got on the microphone and invited anyone who wanted prayer to come forward to the altar. A holy riot of students bum-rushed the altars. People didn't want to leave; they were afraid that they might miss something awesome. Prayers and cries could be heard in classrooms, dorm rooms, and even public campus spots.

News of the revival spread in newspapers and on television. People started pouring into the Asbury auditorium from all over to get into this God-saturated atmosphere. The school dismissed all classes. Their 1,500-capacity auditorium was packed out with standing-room-only crowds.

People skeptical of the move came to see and ended up weeping at the altar and confessing their sin. Asbury students went to other churches, campuses, and outreaches and saw a season of "suddenlies" as Heaven broke open over those venues. One student wrote in his diary, "A few moments ago there came a spontaneous movement of the Holy Spirit."[2]

By the end of the week, 12,000 people had come from all over the country to visit the revival. By the summer of 1970, at least 130 colleges and seminaries were rocked by this revival. It became a national movement.

The college remained ground zero for this revival with meetings continuing at night and on weekends. Asbury University had another God invasion in early 2006. The auditorium was filled with prayer, worship, and testimonies of God experiences for days. God can suddenly do it again!

Spontaneity, Surprise, and the Spirit

The wind blows where it wishes, and you hear the sound of it, but cannot tell where it comes from and where it goes. So is everyone who is born of the Spirit (John 3:8).

Finney said that he often went into the pulpit not knowing what he was going to preach and dependent on the Holy Spirit for what to say. He said that these times produced his most powerful messages and his greatest success. His spontaneous words and subject matter would open up to him in a manner that surprised him.

The word *spontaneous* is synonymous with the words *break loose, extemporaneous,* and *irresistible*. Spontaneity is a response that wasn't premeditated; it occurs on the spot. Oftentimes in revival, you don't know what might come next.

J. Edwin Orr, commenting on the Businessmen's Prayer Revival of 1857 said, "First, the most distinguishing characteristic was the spontaneity."[3] He was referring to the fact that men's traditions were thrown to the side, as people couldn't predict how the move or prayer meetings would go.

One of the major resistances to revival is a people who are trapped relying on religious routine. Religious routine is the first thing we grab when the freshness of God's presence dries up. We get to a crossroad where we realize that what we're doing spiritually isn't working. We can either continue with ritualism or connect to the Spirit of God. Walking in the Spirit, and following the finger of God, often defies the predictable.

The Move Is Knocking at Your Door

I've often wondered why believers are often caught off guard when revival breaks forth in their midst. Revival not only surprises darkness; sometimes we have the deer-in-headlights look ourselves. While God is the One who sends revival and performs spiritual resuscitation, He still requires His vessels to create a landing spot for this supernatural cargo.

Have you ever felt strongly that a major release of God is at your threshold, but that people aren't getting what you are seeing? Perhaps you feel like Rhoda announcing that revival was at the door:

> *And as Peter knocked at the door of the gate, a girl named Rhoda came to answer. When she recognized Peter's voice, because of her gladness she did not open the gate, but ran in and announced that Peter stood before the gate. But they said to her, "You are beside yourself!" Yet she kept insisting that it was so. So they said, "It is his angel." Now Peter continued knocking; and when they opened the door and saw him, they were astonished* (Acts 12:13-16).

I wonder how often God sends answers to our prayers only to see them return to Him stamped "Unclaimed." You see, it's one thing for Heaven to let your miracle loose, and it is another thing for you to let it in. How can we take time to pray and position ourselves for revival and not recognize it when it comes knocking?

Here are three possible explanations as to why revival signs may be at the door and we may not know it. First, *there is often a lack of expectation due to past experiences.* The intercessory group at Mary's house was praying, but something must have been missing. If you are praying in faith, your prayer should move you in position to receive the object of your prayers. The Jerusalem crew had met earlier in prayer for the apostle James, but Herod killed James. Maybe, because of that experience, they really weren't anticipating a positive outcome. Now, the disciples were about to lose Peter on the altar of James. We must lay out our expectation and allow substance to come to what we are hoping for despite what the track record may dictate. As emerging revivalists, we can't let stuff get piled on disappointments. Maybe you have asked God to release a move and you haven't felt like anything good came of it. Just remember that, from the human perspective, revivals often come out of nowhere.

The second reason we may not recognize revival at the door is that *we have dumbed down our prayers to religious formalities.* We must see prayer in its truest light of a Heaven-and-earth-moving activity. When we lose sight of a sovereign God whose plans will not be thwarted, we can become overwhelmed by the severity of our situation. So often, darkness wants you caught up in going through the motions of prayer instead of really prevailing. God doesn't box you in, but it takes faith in God's name to bust you out. You can't pray for revival like you bless your microwavable mac-and-cheese; you must contend. So often what is needed is urgency and desperation in our secret place.

The third reason we may miss the signs of revival is that *we are busy trying to master our plan rather than getting the Master's plan.* It's quite possible that these prayer warriors had their own ideas as to how to bust Peter loose, but it didn't include a sovereign act of the Almighty. Maybe they thought Herod had to die first. So many erroneously believe that there has to be an administration change before we can have revival. The greatest obstacle to fresh discovery is not ignorance, but the illusion of knowledge. We often feel that there's no other way but the way that it has happened for someone else. So, when Peter knocked and Rhoda told them, the early Church was more willing to believe that it was Peter's angel, rather than that Peter was alive. Wicked Herod would later die due to judgment, but God had a Master plan to spring Peter.

I'm recruiting you to be a part of the Rhoda Company. She represents a forerunner that remains sensitive to the signs of God's release while serving. Perhaps her most significant asset in turning this saga around was her persistence. Right after being accused of being just south of berserk, the Bible notes, *"Yet, she kept insisting that it was so"* (Acts 12:15). It's going to take faith to convince others that a move of God is imminent and at our doorstep. My favorite part of this whole story is that Rhoda didn't go to the door and bring back Peter; she kept insisting until they heard the knock themselves. The Word says, *"When they opened the door and saw him, they were astonished"* (Acts 12:16). Rhoda was a sign to them. A sign refuses to be ignored or overlooked. That's exactly how revival still surprises those you wouldn't expect it to. Some of the people who appear expectant are really not.

Grab Hold of a Lunch or Grab Hold of a Legacy

Today, New York City is a global city, with headquarters for the UN, commerce, culture, research, and entertainment. Just over 150 years ago, New York City was eerily similar to what it is today—fast-paced, diverse, financially driven, and irreligious. It also was eyeing an economic downturn that saw the bottom fall out.

Fred W. Hoffman wrote:

Greedy speculation, excessive railroad development and a wildcat currency system combined to bring about an unexpected collapse in the financial structure of the nation. Hundreds of banks failed...business houses were forced to close their doors. Factories were shut down... Stripped of the self-dependence and in despair men again found time to think on their need of God.[4]

In 1857, churches were in decline and thousands were disillusioned with Christianity. The city had its fair share of empty church buildings. In 1856, William Arthur published a book that ended with a cry to God to "crown this nineteenth century with a revival of 'pure and undefiled religion,' greater than...any 'demonstration of the Spirit' ever vouchsafed to man."[5]

Within one year that cry was answered with the Businessman's Prayer Revival of 1857. A churchgoer, Jeremiah Lamphier became desperate to see a major move of God reverse the dark trends that New York was experiencing. Lamphier had been dramatically saved in Charles Finney's church 15 years earlier.

In July 1857, Lamphier began to hand out tracts and visit people who lived around his church. He was a soul winner and eventually emerged as the catalyst for one of the greatest revivals this nation has ever seen.

Lamphier would watch business people during their lunch hour and could discern the stress, heartache, and emptiness in their countenance. Suddenly, the idea came to him to offer midday spiritual refreshment by starting a prayer meeting. He first got approval from his church to host a noontime prayer meeting. He set a date, September 23, for his first prayer meeting on the third floor of his church on Fulton Street.

Lamphier showed up early and anxious for his first noon prayer meeting. At 12:00, no one showed up. Minutes seemed like hours as Lamphier prayed by himself—not even his church members showed up. For at least 20 minutes, there was no movement and no masses. Somewhere between 20 and 30 minutes after the hour, a single individual showed up to pray. In three weeks, this meeting grew until there were 100 men crying out for their city and a saturation of God to impact lives.

Within a month, pastors who had come to Fulton Street to cry out started morning prayer meetings all over the city. Overflow crowds caused people to meet in stores, police departments, and local venues. Newspapers began to report on this, and within several months prayer meetings had risen up in other major cities—Boston, Washington DC, St. Louis, Denver, Chicago, New Orleans, and a host of other cities.

Eventually, because of lack of business, shops shut down between the hours of 11:00 and 2:00. Jesus was the topic of conversation everywhere. By spring of 1857, over 6,000 people met daily for prayer in New York City. You would find hundreds in the street not able to find room inside to pray. All of a sudden, people started witnessing and winning people to Christ, and the revival was fully on. At a certain point in this revival, 50,000 a week were coming to Christ. During this time of recession, the crime rate surprisingly dropped. Soon, other cities started reaping some serious fruit and seeing numbers come to Christ. In 1858, a tent revival started in Philadelphia that lasted four months and saw 10,000 conversions. It was reported that in some New England towns everybody got saved.

In the NYC harbor, there was a battleship called *North Carolina* with over 1,000 men anchored in it. Four young Christian sailors decided to start a prayer meeting. Once, the Holy Spirit fell and they got loud in their praise and prayer, so other sailors came below to ridicule and taunt them but ended up converted. The meetings continued daily with hundreds saved. The revival had a cloud that affected people on land or on sea. In the New England area, this move of God impacted college students as well. Yale University was significantly impacted by this wind of the Spirit to the point that it was impossible to estimate the number of conversions. Amherst College got Holy Ghost aftershocks and spiritual tremors to the point that the president of the college declared that practically every member of the student body had gotten saved. Edwin Orr estimated that one million were converted out of a population of less than 30 million within a two-year period between 1858 and 1859.

No Run of the Mill, After-School Revival Meetings

Recently, I did a conference in Manteca, California, with hundreds of young adults. I spoke on revivals and the powerful influence of a single-focused life. In that crowd sat Chris Scoz, a senior at Manteca High. He represents how a move of God can hit anywhere and through people who may surprise you. At 15, while being homeschooled, he felt God impress upon him that he would only have a short window to impact a high school. So in the fall of his junior year, Chris decided to go to Manteca High. That summer, he grabbed other students to completely douse the campus in prayer. They prayed over every locker that God would break re-bellion and demonstrate His power. There was a Christian club on campus, but it had folded due to lack of interest. But God can turn autopsies into awakenings! As Ernest Baker, author of *Revivals in the Bible*, said, "The Revivals of Christianity have occurred when the funeral of faith has seemed high."[6]

In April of Chris's junior year, he felt led to resurrect the Christian club, but with a twist—he believed it should be a revival club. Manteca High has about 1,400 students and has the same problems of every other high school. Chris felt that Heaven's vision for his campus was to demonstrate His love and raise up a movement that would model something for high schools all over. In two months, the revival club went from 10 students to 50 students. There were students who did drugs and a Buddhist student who got saved. Healings also occurred.

That summer, Chris sensed God was telling him that revival would come to Manteca High School and spread to the other high schools of the area. He called for a 21-day fast among students to start off his senior year. They met in the quad with a handful of students, crying out after school for an outpouring. These students were not distracted with iPods; they just had broken hearts for their peers to meet Jesus. Suddenly, there came acceleration to the fire. Their first meeting was 30 young people in a classroom, but they quickly outgrew it. It became 60-80 students in the cafeteria, and now it is 120-plus students that meet in the high school theater.

Chris has an evangelist's heart with a prophetic gifting. His next idea was a healing tent to pray for the sick. They even start off their Friday Revival Club, not with music, but with healing the sick. Chris and other high school revivalists step out with words of knowledge and invite the sick to come up and get prayer. They have seen scoliosis healed, vision restored, cysts disappear, asthma leave, and a medically verified hole in a heart close up. Just recently a Muslim student was healed of a broken jaw on the spot!

This miracle happened in front of other students outside the theater. Remember, these are young adults praying for young adults. One of Chris's right-hand guys is a young man who got saved and delivered from cocaine addiction at one of these meetings. After inviting the sick to get healed, Chris or another student preaches the Word, and it all ends with an altar call.

Most recently, Chris and the team started a campus prayer room and a discipleship program. The miracles have drawn atheists, "emo" teenagers, and others to come out weekly. They have also started to do revival clubs on other campuses in the area. Only God could take a homeschooled teen in his sophomore year and bring revival within such a short time. The best-kept secret is one the ACLU cannot stop, and it's happening right underneath our noses on public high school campuses. Students are tired of being told what they are not and have started to believe God for what can be…revival!

9

Becoming a Mouthpiece of an Awakening

And it shall come to pass afterward that I will pour out My Spirit on all flesh; your sons and your daughters shall prophesy, your old men shall dream dreams, your young men shall see visions. And also on My menservants and on My maidservants I will pour out My Spirit in those days. ...And it shall come to pass that whoever calls on the name of the Lord shall be saved. For in Mount Zion and in Jerusalem there shall be deliverance, as the Lord has said, among the remnant whom the Lord calls (Joel 2:28-29,32).

Joel's prophecy stated that when an outpouring hits, *"Your sons and your daughters shall prophesy."* Revivals always cause vessels to declare the counsel of God to their generation. Revivals bring about a prophetic culture that hungers to know what God is currently saying. In history, a prophetic Church always emerged after an outpouring of the Holy Ghost. Part of the reason for this is that in revivals God exceptionally reveals Himself. Revelation becomes a booster to faith and boldness, causing a vessel to be more in tune with the eternal than the temporal.

The following passages attest to the fact that the proclamation of power and a prophetic mouthpiece will play a major part in the revival of the end times:

Behold, I will send you Elijah the prophet before the coming of the great and dreadful day of the Lord (Malachi 4:5).

Malachi's prophecy that the Spirit of Elijah is coming was never meant to have one solitary appearance in John the Baptist. This fiery spirit accompanies every true revival, culminating in an ultimate appearance in the generation when Jesus returns.

The original Elijah became the prophet of coming rain and became one of the most significant mouthpieces of God in the Old Testament. This generation will operate in the spirit of Elijah as John the Baptist did, who will prepare hearts for the ultimate move of God (the coming of the Messiah).

Types of Prophetic Mouthpieces in an Awakening

The mouthpiece is a proclaimer of God's prophetic standard. In times of God's visitation, there are John the Baptists who call God's people back to Book-of-Acts Christianity. Their message is one of holiness, consecration, and necessary preparation. Their fuel is brought on by both their encounters with God and their vision of what's coming. Sometimes they may be identified as an intercessor or a collaborator to a person known as the "face of revival." Frank Bartleman was used in the Azusa Street Revival in this capacity, and of course, John the Baptist modeled being a mouthpiece for Jesus. These individuals are so gripped and extreme that many are not ready to receive their message.

The mouthpiece becomes a prophetic interpreter of the awakening. This feature is acutely needed in moves where God does a new thing, for it facilitates understanding of the unexplainable aspects of a revival. Peter told the crowd at Jerusalem, who thought the upper room inhabitants were drunk, *"This is that which was spoken of by the prophet Joel"* (Acts 2:16 KJV). I like the fact that Peter cleared up the fact that they weren't drunk, but Peter's genius was that he connected this move to the prophets they already all believed. This mouthpiece must be part theologian and part son of Issachar (the tribe that understood their times and knew what Israel ought to do—see 1 Chronicles 12:32).

Jonathan Edwards was a theologian and a major mouthpiece in the First Great Awakening. He wrote *A Treatise Concerning Religious Affections* answering so many questions on discerning what were legitimate manifestations. Many people shook, rattled, and rolled in his meetings under conviction, so he interpreted these phenomena and helped spiritual neophytes track with the move of God.

The mouthpiece becomes a prophetic trumpet call to recognize and radiate righteousness. This differs from the first type of mouthpiece in that this type of mouthpiece challenges more in the midst of the revival, whereas the first challenges people at the beginning of a revival. This mouthpiece doesn't allow the masses to take the movement for granted. These individuals continually point out the purpose of the refreshing and keep the big picture before the people. God gives us an experience to carry us to our purpose, but the enemy wants us to make the experience our purpose. An example of this is King Jehoshaphat in his Old Testament revival. In order to conserve the results of revival, he sent out teachers and Levites to give instructions from God's Word throughout all the cities (see 2 Chron. 9). Jehoshaphat called people to recognize and radiate righteousness.

The mouthpiece becomes a prophetic roar against societal injustices. Revival is a divine attack against darkness. Often revivals become the answer to a social injustice. Revivalists have spoken up for the injustices of women's suffrage, child labor abuses, slavery, and sex-trade trafficking. William Wilberforce was a British politician serving in parliament. He contended for revival of the Church, and even wrote a book on revival, believing that this would make for a unified society. He spoke against the modern vices of his day, including excessive drinking, immorality, and lewdness. Yet, he is most known as a benchmark abolitionist. His hatred for the slavery of Africans was renowned. He ultimately got the Anti-Slavery Society off the ground and his campaign led to the Slavery Abolition Act of 1833, which abolished slavery in most of the British Empire. Once again, we need a prophetic roar against the oppression and injustices of our day!

The mouthpiece becomes a prophetic evangelist who speaks to the lost. These vessels become the voice of God's redemptive purpose. Their minds are awake to the soul's need for salvation. Like Philip, one of the first to take revival beyond Jerusalem, these mouthpieces are instrumental in unleashing an awakening into the surrounding region. Often, without the Philips ready to step out from the revival meetings to meet with those outside, revivals don't move from micro-revival to awakening. If revival is kept inside church walls, it will wither up. Ladies and gentlemen, revival must leave the building. This next revival will require thousands upon thousands of mouthpieces who will get the message out.

Wigglesworth and the God Zone

Smith Wigglesworth is referred to as the Apostle of Faith. He was used mightily in extraordinary miracles. Smith was a man of compassion and lived the lifestyle of a soul winner. His first convert was his mother, Maria Wigglesworth.

At one point, Smith received an invitation to come and minister in New Zealand. He went in 1922, and was hosted by a pastor named H. Roberts, who was greatly burdened for revival in his homeland. Wigglesworth wasn't really known in New Zealand, and Pastor Roberts' decision to financially cover the expenses seemed risky. But these meetings quickly began to grow. Each meeting experienced a stronger release of the presence of God. Miraculous healings took place, deformities and diseases left the bodies of young people, and those who witnessed it wept.

The third night was packed with a full-capacity crowd of 3,000; at least 1,000 were turned away due to a lack of room. The local newspaper headlined, "Faith Healing Extraordinary Scenes at Town Hall—the Deaf Made to Hear," which kicked the interest into overdrive. Then Smith began to have meetings in other areas. In one meeting, an 11-year-old who was paralyzed got up and walked as his father wept. In one night 500 got saved, and over 2,000 came to Christ in the whole campaign. People were also making restitution if they had stolen or defrauded anyone.

Smith not only saw people saved in these meetings, but also outside, as he was an everywhere evangelist. Wigglesworth would say, "I would sooner have one soul saved, than 10,000 healed," and "I preach and practice healing to attract the people just as our Lord did." Wigglesworth was single-handedly responsible for launching the Pentecostal movement in the country of New Zealand. Even many great admirers of Wigglesworth don't know that he would often hit the streets telling people about Jesus. Every day his cry was to win souls and to be a voice of redemption in many lives.

From Atheist to Revivalist

Charles Finney had such a profound impact during the Second Great Awakening that he has been called the Father of Modern Revivalism. Finney was the son of a farmer, and his leadership gifts caused him to stand out in his hometown. He studied as an apprentice to become a lawyer and was regarded in Jefferson County as a most eligible bachelor. Finney was known to argue against the existence of God until he had a supernatural revelation that converted him. One night, he came under a serious sense of conviction from the Holy Spirit. The next day, a voice started speaking to him and the Gospel opened up to him. Instead of going to the office, he went into the woods and cried out for mercy. There, he told the Lord that he would preach the Gospel if God would consume him.

Holy boldness and revival fires immediately followed his life as he shared his testimony. His whole mind and heart were taken up with Jesus, and no earthly thing could compete with winning souls and becoming God's mouthpiece. From the first time Finney opened his mouth for Christ, people were coming under conviction and getting saved. At dinner at a local's house, Finney was blessing the food and a professed Universalist ran from the table and locked himself in a room, only to emerge saved.

When Charles Finney opened his mouth, he was dropping nuclear weaponry on darkness. His convictions were forged in the furnace of revival. To reach as many people as possible, Finney innovated "new measures." Among the most objectionable were: daily services over a series of days, use of "street talk" by the preacher, the "anxious bench" for convicted seekers, and praying for people by name. None of these things seem extreme now, but they triggered consternation among the established clergy of his day. Later, Finney was ordained in the Presbyterian Church in 1824 and began missionary labors in upper New York.

At Evan Mills, Finney was bothered that the people said they were "pleased" with his sermons. So he decided to increase the voltage of his messages by stressing the need for conversion. At the conclusion of his message, he stepped out with a daring move: he gave an altar call! Nobody stood. The next night the entire town came out, including an angry man with a gun intending to kill the evangelist. When he finished his message and gave the altar call, dozens stood, and many fell out in the power and groaned. The man with the gun changed his mind. Finney continued for a series of nights, with many getting saved. He rode from town to town, seeing a spirit of revival seize communities that were thought to be burnt out on Christianity.

Finney went to Antwerp, Belgium, but there weren't too many Christians. Finney met with violent opposition from the atheistic, anti-God crowd. Neighbors took the wheels off his carriage as he was passing by on the Sabbath. The residents of Antwerp had nicknamed one neighborhood "Sodom" because it so resembled the corruption of the biblical city. Finney was invited to hold an afternoon service in this neighborhood. Without having natural knowledge of its reputation, Finney was led to preach on the verse, *"Get up, get out of this place; for the Lord will destroy this city!"* vividly describing the condition of Sodom. Nearly the entire crowd almost simultaneously fell upon their knees crying out for their souls. Finney had an evening appointment and left, but many of the people stayed all night and had to be carried home in the morning because they were so overcome with conviction and God's presence.

When Finney went to Rome, New York, God so seized the folks with genuine conviction that Finney was concerned that the people couldn't control their emotions. He tried to be extra calm in the altar prayer, but the crowd had begun to convulse violently. Revival services went on for three weeks with people running to attend; ministers came from nearby towns to experience what was going on. So many people got saved in these services, in homes, and in businesses that it was impossible to keep up. Some mockers would get drunk all day and condemn the revival, until one of them fell down dead. After that, nearly all of the adult population of Rome was brought into the Kingdom. It was said that everyone who came to Rome felt an overwhelming sense of God's presence.

In Rochester, New York, the Holy Spirit came in incredible power. Rochester was a metropolis situated next to the newly finished Erie Canal. Finney began to make use of "the anxious seat" in the front of the church for people desiring salvation. God began to do a work among the city's professionals. Lawyers, doctors, and businessmen were getting radically saved. Wesley Duewel wrote:

> A skeptic had a large, flourishing high school in Rochester. A number of the students attended the Finney meetings and became deeply convicted. In fact, the entire business district often shut down to be at his meetings. The prosecuting attorney of Rochester even got saved in the revival. Great crowds followed Finney as he moved from church to church. Many said that it was the greatest local revival in American History.[1]

Minister and author Dr. Henry Ward Beecher said, "The nation-wide revival sparked by Rochester was the greatest work of God, and the greatest revival of religion that the world has ever seen in so short a time."[2] Part of the reason for this extraordinary revival was the outstanding spirit of intercession that invaded the region. A church leader deeply convicted of his own sins sobbed aloud as he walked down the street. This man got right with God and became Finney's prayer partner. The population of Rochester tripled after the revival, but the crime rate decreased by two-thirds!

Profile of an Emerging Revivalist

An emerging revivalist is gripped by holy dreams. In order to successfully catalyze a mighty spiritual awakening, you must envision God's blueprint for your world. God's dreams are not limited to ecstatic realms alone, but live in the revolutionary realm that creates a new reality. Mark Shaw, author of *Global Awakening*, said, "Prior to the outbreak of a revival people in a given context feel that their maps of reality no longer work. The old ways appear to be dead ends."[3] Revivalists dream the dreams of redemption. They see things off in a distance that ignite movement in them and eventually in all those who get around them. It's easy to look around and feel powerless to bring change to the world around us. I believe the powerless feeling is more common now than ever. Difficult places and tough times make for tough vessels and true revivalists.

In First Samuel 13 and 14, Jonathan had to envision a holy dream or his nation would have been doomed. The Philistines had surrounded God's children and had taken possession of all weapons but one sword. King Saul was under a pomegranate tree in Migron with 600 defenseless soldiers—before the Philistines had attacked them, he had had 3,000. Saul's army was definitely in decline mode and his spiritual and visionary stagnation weren't going to attract anybody anytime soon. But Jonathan visualized a move of God that would get his people back to their legacy and standard as God's victorious and chosen children:

> *Now it happened one day that Jonathan the son of Saul said to the young man who bore his armor, "Come, let us go over to the Philistines' garrison that is on the other side." But he did not tell his father. And Saul was sitting in the outskirts of Gibeah under a pomegranate tree which is in Migron. The people who were with him were about six hundred men* (1 Samuel 14:1-2).

Revivalists, who capture Heaven's holy dreams, are emboldened to cross over the lines that darkness has drawn in their generation. Meanwhile, the religious crowd gets marginalized like Saul did. Religionists love to get under the shady trees of the sidelines, where they don't have anything disturbing or exciting going on. But revivalists reject being mere spectators, sidelined in safe confines. They jump in the battle for their generation.

Emerging revivalists are possessed by God. Our Christian experience should be a passionate, sacrificial devotion to Christ. It was said that the early Christians conquered because they outlived and out-died their adversaries. They showed a quality of life that was impossible apart from Jesus. A revivalist must allow Jesus to be his or her only explanation. What else could account for the large spiritual craters left by Savonarola, Christmas Evans, Zinzendorf, and others? Great opportunities often lie in doing the opposite of what everyone else is doing, and those who win the world cannot be afraid to come in conflict with it.

Jonathan ran toward the Philistines, while Saul ran from them. The Philistines had taken the blacksmiths away so the Israelites could not get armed. Mario Murillo says, "The greatest sin of modern Christianity is the pursuit of a comfortable Christian life." Revival is God's radical measure to get the Church at a given time back to normal before it falls into spiritual oblivion and irrelevance. When we model a brand of Christianity that does not pack passion and power, then we are modeling a watered-down product.

Jonathan recruited his armor bearer to go with him and attack the Philistines. The Philistines had 30,000 swords and occupied the higher ground. Jonathan's plan was not only dangerous; it was absurd. Jonathan was a kid with one sword—nobody even noticed that he had gone. Nobody had given him a single chance that his act of faith could change the course of a nation. Jonathan's plan was to reveal himself to the Philistines and, if the Philistines told Jonathan to come up, he would lead his armies to attack, knowing that God had delivered the enemy over to him. Wow! Personally, I would have wanted a bigger confirmation that Heaven had my back. But Jonathan didn't need some big sign to rise up for a revolution—he was the sign! It's as if he was saying, "We go unless we get a 'No!'" I wonder how Christianity has become a stay-unless-you-feel-led-to-go movement. It didn't start out that way!

Emerging revivalists move from the mundane to the miraculous. Some people read history, some people are history, and some people make history. History makers are people who don't wait for the perfect conditions. They go and create the conditions they want. The Christian life is primarily about spiritual transformation through spiritual power, manifested in a spiritual community, that impacts the larger community. Leonard Ravenhill says, "Revival is when God gets so sick and tired of being misrepresented that He shows Himself."

Jonathan moved from the category called overwhelming to the one called overcoming. After being challenged by the Philistines, he began to climb up on his hands and knees with his armor bearer after him:

> *And Jonathan climbed up on his hands and knees with his armorbearer after him; and they fell before Jonathan. And as he came after him, his armor bearer killed them. That first slaughter which Jonathan and his armor bearer made was about twenty men within about half an acre of land. And there was trembling in the camp, in the field, and among all the people. The garrison and the raiders also trembled; and the earth quaked, so that it was a very great trembling. Now the watchmen of Saul in Gibeah of Benjamin looked, and there was the multitude, melting away; and they went here and there (1 Samuel 14:13-16).*

Jonathan moved up a mountain totally exposed and vulnerable in the natural, yet he believed that God would intervene and win the day. He was spot on! As Jonathan and his armor bearer took out 20 men in a half-acre of land, God joined in and released an earthquake that caused the enemies to tremble. In every Christian exploit there are always the human and the divine, the sword of the Lord and Gideon (see Judg. 7:18). We must, like Jonathan, press in for the miraculous and then expect the supernatural to manifest.

Emerging revivalists operate from a deeper level of sensitivity to God and audacity to resistance. You must set your face like flint toward the sweeping transformation of your life. A deep awareness of the presence was the secret of great revivalists of the past. This consciousness breaks off the fear of man and rejection from an explosive vessel of God. George Whitefield had dead cats thrown on him as he preached. Howell Harris of Wales had to escape people wanting to beat him up. None of these threats deterred them. Every move of God requires an accompanying move by a bold servant of God. Saul was waiting passively for his breakthrough, while Jonathan sensed the urge to break through in his spirit. Once Jonathan began his attempts to recover territory, God gave him his entire nation back.

Apostle Paul was sensitive enough to cancel the "psychic-friends hotline" off the air when he cast the devil out of the young girl in Philippi (see Acts 16:16-18). Though he went to jail unjustly, Paul was tender enough to praise God and see a revival in a prison house. Finally, he was bold enough to demand an official escort by the dignitaries when he left town. Like Paul, we are not supposed to leave quietly. We must make some holy commotion before we leave a place (see Acts 16:35-40).

Emerging revivalists become the incarnation of their revelation. Moses desired God's presence and to experience His glory above everything else. Moses also became the incarnation of his revelation—he became a burning one after encountering the burning bush. This incarnation dynamic is key, because the vessel communicates from every aspect of his or her being. He or she cannot be shut up or shut down. Revivals typically don't fall on an unprepared people. We need John the Baptists calling for a revolution, looking like a poster child for radical revolutionaries with a camel-skin vest, eating a grasshopper quesadilla with honey mustard sauce dripping from it. God's holy agents aren't secret; they just know the secret to influence and impact.

Emerging Revivalists
Invite Heaven's Invasion

Angela is a new-breed emerging revivalist. When she was a student at her university, she walked with a holy dream in her heart. Angela had heard of the visitation of God that her university had experienced almost two decades earlier, and she was definitely gripped for another move. She wasn't going to sit on the sidelines and allow any excuses or resistance to derail her. So she began to ask what it would take to start a campus movement. Angela was told she had to fill out an application from the Associated Student's office. She started a Bible study and had enough students involved to fill out the necessary officers. They prayed for their campus and an awakening among the students.

When Angela got into the office, she knew she needed favor to get permission to be a recognized group. Angela asked the Holy Spirit for help and received a word of knowledge that the gal who was helping her was having respiratory problems. So Angela stepped out, defying the hindrance of being appropriate, and shared the word with the gal. The word was right on, and the gal was surprised and asked Angela how she knew. Angela told her it was Jesus and asked if she could pray for her. As they were praying, Angela said, "Someone around you has been operating in witchcraft. You have had headaches and haven't been able to sleep at night." The gal said it was all true, and that her mom was a Wiccan. As this gal got healed, she gave her life to the Lord, and Angela got her paperwork filed for the group status. This breakthrough is personally meaningful to me as I was in that "visitation" two decades earlier on that very campus.

Every Witch Way but Loose

Angela was excited about her new favor and the release to run with God's dream. Then she started getting attacked and felt it was unique. She started seeing a woman dressed in black cross her path and noticed some strange things going on. After some prayer, she felt that it was a spirit of witchcraft coming against her.

New-breed revivalists always see darkness pull out all stops to discourage them, but in the end darkness pulls out. Helen Blavatsky, considered the mother of the modern spiritualist movement, came to America from Russia in the 1800s. She popularized mediums and psychics in NYC at the height of the spiritualist craze hitting the nation. She connected with the Eddy brothers, who displayed dark psychic abilities, and together with another occultist, Henry Olcott, they founded the Theosophical Society in 1875. But they made a serious mistake of moving into the same neighborhood as Charles Finney. At the time, Finney was holding nightly overflowing prayer meetings and seeing powerful demonstrations of the Holy Spirit and numerous conversions. The enemy probably thought that the spirit of witchcraft would hinder the revival, but it was the occult whose plug got pulled. Soon thereafter, Blavatsky and Olcott got out of Dodge, moved to India, and were eventually discredited.

Angela had some friends tell her maybe she was biting off too much with all the "Christian stuff" she was doing. So Angela asked the Holy Spirit what she should do. Her instructions were to go down to the local occult store because she had an assignment there. Angela walked inside the occult store, and guess who was behind the counter? It was the woman dressed in black who had been crossing Angela's path so much recently. There was also a nicely dressed business lady, who was complaining about getting a bad "reading" from the witch lady. Angela quickly asked the Lord for a word for the businesswoman. Angela approached her and told her that her brothers had rejected her while they were growing up.

Sensing the connection, Angela invited the lady to step outside and proceeded to tell her two more things that no one else knew. The business lady started crying and said she went to churches but never experienced the power of God till that moment. Angela prayed with her as she gave her life to the Lord. This business lady also started coming to Angela's newly official Bible group. I believe that Angela represents many revivalists who will shake campuses in this coming move of revival. Fasten your safety belts and get ready for Heaven to bust loose over your life and cross some lines.

10

Mainstreaming the Miraculous: Now *This* I've Got to See!

Revival is the exchange of the form of godliness for its living power.—John Bonar

Burning Bushes and Burning Ones

We see signs of a restless state of mind all around us. People are edgy and seemingly agitated over the smallest things. But becoming restless is not all bad. In fact, it might be God in some cases. Restlessness is used by God to prepare us for holy invasions, and it usually precedes a powerful touch in a person's life. Ron Hutchcraft says, "God made you restless for more because He wants to eternalize your life, to make it count for that which will last forever."[1]

The children of Israel were brought out of Egypt by the combination weaponry of revival and miracles. The plagues were miraculous demonstrations that weakened Pharaoh and Egypt and revealed Israel's God. Before they exited Egypt, the Israelites had to be brought to a revitalized faith and obedience to God or else they wouldn't have left. Hebrews 11:29 says, *"By faith they passed through the Red sea as by dry land…."* This required a revived mindset from the newly freed captives.

James A. Stewart wrote: "Any movement that fails to deliver the local church from its subnormal existence and raise it to a higher elevated position in its ascended Lord has no true mark of a New Testament Revival."[2] The saga of revival contains the Reviver and the Revivalist—the burning bush and the burning ones.

Initially, Moses was more of a burned-out one than the human torch he would later become. He had dreams of his people being revived, freed from oppression, and rising up into their promised inheritance. But 40 years had passed since there was any smoke coming off Moses' faith. Little did he know that one encounter with God makes His ministers *"flames of fire"* (Heb. 1:7) and would change everything:

> *And the Angel of the Lord appeared to him in a flame of fire from the midst of a bush. So he looked, and behold, the bush was burning with fire, but the bush was not consumed. Then Moses said, "I will now turn aside and see this great sight, why the bush does not burn." So when the Lord saw that he turned aside to look, God called to him from the midst of the bush and said, "Moses, Moses!" And he said, "Here I am." And the Lord said: "I have surely seen the oppression of My people who are in Egypt, and have heard their cry because of their taskmasters, for I know their sorrows. So I have come down to deliver them out of the hand of the Egyptians, and to bring them up from that land to a good and large land…"* (Exodus 3:2-4,7-8).

Imagine walking along your typical route and stumbling upon a Ripley's-Believe-It-Or-Not! shrub that is on fire without smoke or charred branches. This Old Testament "Unsolved Mystery" caught Moses' attention and drew him in. When Moses saw this he said, *"I will now turn aside and see this great sight...."*

You have to begin to recognize prophetic signs and the divine promptings Heaven uses to draw you in. Prophetic signs show you that a divine moment is ripe to be seized. We must learn to watch for signs of God's activity around us and perceive when God is arranging for us to join Him. Revelations are not for the unobservant. God will give us vision, but we must be somewhat attuned to His movement. In some ways, Moses was looking at what God was going to turn him into. Here was an ordinary wilderness shrub carrying a fuel-less fire that forced you to recognize it and reckon with it.

The Body of Christ gravely needs an encounter with the fire in this new millennium. Experiencing the fire of God's presence will bring back a holy awe, which will thrust us forth with new boldness. The sheer fire of God's presence can also bring serious wake-up calls to sinners. In revivals, one of the foremost hallmarks of a spiritual awakening is a penetrating consciousness of God's holiness and presence.

Qualities of the Fire of the Eternal One

1) The fire brings a sobering and gripping awareness of the awesomeness of God.

2) The fire brings a complete captivation of heart and soul.

3) The fire brings a righteous radioactivity that spreads from a carrier to others.

4) The fire creates a combustible intensity and holy horsepower that doesn't exhaust before resistance.

5) The fire doesn't need an approving atmosphere in order to burn.

A fresh baptism of fire is awaiting you. An unprecedented encounter with the Eternal Flame of God is hovering over you right now. This shekinah bush called Moses out of obscurity and into history. Revivals often call individuals out of mundane occupations and thrust them into remarkable ministry posts.

Here was a revivalist needing to be revived:

Then Moses answered and said, "But suppose they will not believe me or listen to my voice; suppose they say, 'The Lord has not appeared to you.' So the Lord said to him, "What is that in your hand?" He said, "A rod." And He said, "Cast it on the ground." So he cast it on the ground, and it became a serpent; and Moses fled from it. Then the Lord said to Moses, "Reach out your hand and take it by the tail" (and he reached out his hand and caught it, and it became a rod in his hand), "that they may believe that the Lord God of their fathers, the God of Abraham, the God of Isaac, and the God of Jacob, has appeared to you" (Exodus 4:1-5).

Moses recognized the difficulty in bringing the divine message given him. He foresaw that getting the children of Israel to believe was one thing, but getting Pharaoh to comply was completely different. Moses knew that he needed some heavenly credentials for a perceived credibility gap. After acknowledging the rod in Moses' hand, the Lord told him to cast it on the ground. The next thing God exposed the emerging revivalist to was danger—a serpent—but he needed to learn something vital to revivals. Overcoming a hindrance usually precedes advancement in the Kingdom and in revival. Then God told Moses to take the serpent by the tail—not the way you should usually grab a poisonous reptile. But Moses had to see the supernatural power and authority God was giving him.

Why does the supernatural realm so often accompany revivals? The world and the spiritually frozen both need to see the endorsement of God to fully surrender. There's a credibility gap that must be addressed for the billions of people who cover the earth.

For many, great preaching alone won't convince the masses, while a miracle often settles the issue. We must have demonstration and power. We need fire to fall to thaw cold hearts.

Even When You Least Expect It, It's Christmas Time

In *Cataracts of Revival*, G.J. Morgan writes about revivalist Christmas Evans:

> It came after Christmas Evans, the Welsh preacher, had spent three hours in a wood, waiting upon God in prayer, broken with sorrow, because he felt his spiritual life very low and cold. "I was weary," he says, referring to this period, "of a cold heart in the pulpit, in secret prayer and in the study...I soon felt the fetters loosening and the old hardness of heart softening and I thought, mountains of frost and snow dissolving and melting within me... On the following day I preached with such power to a vast concourse of people gathered on the hillside that a revival broke out that day and spread through the whole Principality."[3]

Evans suffered the death of his father when he was nine years old and was left dirt-poor. He spent his next six years with an abusive uncle, who made Evans a farm servant. At 17, Evans couldn't read a word. A minister took him under his wing, and Evans got saved at a revival. Some of Evans' old buddies got so mad that they jumped him one dark night and beat him so bad that he lost sight in one of his eyes. On the night he lost his eye, he had a night vision of judgment day, and it gave him an intense desire to preach Christ. In spite of everything the enemy threw at Evans, he became one of the greatest revivalists in Wales. His secret was his prayer life and the fire he encountered when he got saved.

Christmas Evans unexpectedly exploded onto the scene in 1794. A big open-air festival drew a large mass of people near Llanelly. It was the event of the year, but the headlining preacher didn't show up. Many ministers were approached on the spot but bowed out. Timothy Thomas, the man who baptized Evans, was asked to substitute preach, but he too declined and volunteered the unknown, poorly dressed, lanky, disfigured Christmas Evans. He was not the "big name" preacher anyone would have chosen for this huge occasion, but God scripts history differently. As Evans got off to an awkward start, people walked off to get refreshments. Then all of a sudden, Heaven's fire hit that field. People started to cry and shouts were let out. People were asking, "Who is this guy?" and soon would never forget him.

His preaching started what later became known as the Welsh Revival of the 18th century. Thousands were saved as the power of God shook the country. People were so affected by his preaching that they broke out and literally danced for joy. As a result, they were called the "Welsh Jumpers." Others said the people seemed like the inhabitants of a city shaken by an earthquake; they would rush into the streets, falling upon the ground, screaming and calling upon God.

Warren Wiersbe writes:

When asked about style and delivery, Evans said, "Preach the Gospel of the grace of God intelligently, affectionately, and without shame…Let the preacher influence himself; let him reach his own heart, if he would reach the hearts of others; if he would have others feel, he must feel himself."[4]

Christmas Evans said, "Revival is God bending down to the dying embers of a fire just about to go out and breathing into it until it bursts once again into flame." God is currently scheduling your appointment with *fire* and is allowing things to heat up around you. This is exactly how Moses' burning bush turned him into a burning one and launched one of the greatest defeats of darkness over a nation of all time. Fire carries the ability to compel and transform all that it touches.

Hanging With Him and the Seraphim

Isaiah was transformed by encountering the Eternal Flame, leading to his radical volunteerism for a holy epic assignment:

> *Then one of the seraphim flew to me, having in his hand a live coal which he had taken with the tongs from the altar. And he touched my mouth with it, and said: "Behold, this has touched your lips; your iniquity is taken away, and your sin purged." Also I heard the voice of the Lord, saying: "Whom shall I send, and who will go for Us?" Then I said, "Here am I! Send me"* (Isaiah 6:6-8).

A seraphim brought a live coal to touch Isaiah, forever leaving him with a new mark of Heaven. The word seraphim literally means "burning ones." A burning one produces a burning in the lives of others.

A fresh vision of the throne and an encounter goes a long way in the making of a revivalist. We desperately need the live coal from the altar to touch our lives today if we are going to move in the dimension of light needed to transform our world.

When you've grasped the weightiness of God's presence, you won't settle for earthly, lightweight compromises. Isaiah was God's man before he had this experience, but this encounter released him to a new level of consecration and usefulness.

Emerging revivalists must voluntarily rise up to be Heaven's answer. The coming revival will be preceded by revivalists emerging from all sorts of places, burning ones that will actively engage in extending His Kingdom. As strong as it sounds, don't go if you have had no vision of the majesty of God and if you aren't burning for the King. But once you have been touched by fire from

Heaven, you're ready to create a spark that lights up a generation. We're not just hoping for brighter days; we're lighting the match and pouring the oil.

Moses 2.0: A Royal Outlook vs. Situational Mindset

Now you shall speak to him and put the words in his mouth. And I will be with your mouth and with his mouth, and I will teach you what you shall do. So he shall be your spokesman to the people. And he himself shall be as a mouth for you, and you shall be to him as God. And you shall take this rod in your hand, with which you shall do the signs (Exodus 4:15-17).

You would think Moses had been delivered from doubt through the burning bush incident. Yet, God still works with His chosen vessels through the barriers of believing. Here God assures Moses that He will fully equip him for the challenge ahead, and guarantees that he will be instructed at every turn. God promises two vital things to Moses, the emerging revivalist: 1) that he would be like God to Pharaoh, and 2) that he would do signs with his rod. Without divine inspiration and authority before Pharaoh and Egypt, the whole undertaking would have been disastrous.

God asked Moses what was in his hand. God was going to retrofit the simple tool of Moses' trade for darkness-shattering, revival-releasing miracles. God's not depending on what we are but what He can make of us. Moses was in a trying position, sent out upon an assignment in which he hadn't experienced the slightest ounce of success. God was, in essence, telling Moses that he would be clothed in such authority that Pharaoh would be compelled to respect him. Heaven has some upgrades available to you to walk in.

God declared to Moses that the rod was for releasing the miraculous. We must realize that we were created for the supernatural and we become empowered to break oppression off of people. Moses' rod teaches us about knowing with certainty that God has made provision for all the eventualities we will face and that He has already put in us what must be manifested. The rod also teaches us about bringing the sustained environment of righteousness that swallows up the sustained environment of oppression. Once Moses and Aaron arrived in Pharaoh's court demanding that the Hebrews be released, there was resistance. So Moses threw down a rod and it became a serpent. Unimpressed at this point, Pharaoh has his Egyptian magicians perform some clever imitations, leaving multiple serpents on the floor. Yet before all onlookers, Moses' snake swallowed up their snakes.

Paul prophesied that in the Last Days we would be resisted like Moses was resisted in Pharaoh's court:

> *But know this, that in the last days perilous times will come....Now as Jannes and Jambres resisted Moses, so do these also resist the truth: men of corrupt minds, disapproved concerning the faith; but they will progress no further, for their folly will be manifest to all, as theirs also was* (2 Timothy 3:1,8-9).

The false power brokers will be stopped in their tracks and publicly exposed. God always wants to demonstrate His supreme power, especially in revivals and outpourings of the Spirit. We learn from this scene that evil has its limits and God comes to exceed man-made limits. One of my favorite verses to stand on before ministry times is First Corinthians 12:7: *"But the manifestation of the Spirit is given to each one for the profit of all."* We each have been given a "rod," the manifestation of the Spirit, to be a catalyst on this planet to see both revival and awakenings.

Grandmother of the Pentecostal Movement

Maria Woodworth-Etter was born in 1844 in a non-Christian family. When she was 13, her father died. At that time, having committed her life to Christ, she heard God's voice calling her into ministry. However, her church didn't allow women ministers. So Maria resisted that call for two decades, got married, and had kids. She tragically lost five of her six children. Looking for comfort, she clutched the Word of God and discovered that God used women throughout the Scriptures. In 1880 she began her dynamic evangelistic ministry. Though she had strayed from her calling for two decades, that wasn't enough to relegate her to a "Plan B" life. God never gives up on us.

Maria's first opportunity came to preach. As she got up to speak, she had a vision of hell and people ignorant of their danger. Around the clock, she carried this urgency to move people to God. Not too long into her ministry, she felt led to pray for the sick, but she didn't know if it would take away from people getting saved. God made it clear to Maria that praying for the sick would only enhance the lost getting saved. She immediately started seeing the power of God manifest in her meetings with healings, visions, and people coming to Christ.

When Maria preached, the power of God would fall and the lost would run to the altar. Her revival meetings were like a page in the Book of Acts.

In Hartford City, Maria held meetings in a religiously hardened church. In that meeting, people began to weep and the manifestation of the Spirit was evident. The displays of power increased for five weeks. Maria said:

> The power of the Lord, like the wind, swept all over the city, sweeping through the workshops and saloons, arresting sinners of all classes. They fell into trances, had visions of God and got up converted, giving glory to God. Their faces shone like angels and the fear of God fell upon the city. The policemen reported that they had never seen such a dramatic change; crime stopped. A spirit of peace and compassion rested on the city.

There were no fights, nobody cussing and everyone felt God's presence.

One night, at a party 17 miles outside the city, some young ladies thought they would mock the trances in Maria's meetings. They were struck down and laid out as if they had been shot. Their mocking meeting became a prayer meeting as cries for mercy were heard. Scoffers were out in the power all over town. One night, 115 got saved in one altar call. These demonstrations of the Spirit happened in city after city, with the hardest sinners getting saved. In Kokomo, Indiana, Maria had meetings that outdrew Barnum's traveling circus, "The Greatest Show on Earth"—it was upstaged by the divine show from Heaven. The power of God was felt for 50 miles around. Thousands of people got right with God as "marvels and miracles" followed and fell on people.

Revival Healings and Deliverances

There were dramatic miracles of healings. One girl, given up to die by her doctors, was raised off her deathbed after Maria laid hands on her and prayed. Another little girl was carried into the meetings with spinal meningitis. She was completely paralyzed, and it had impaired her brain. In minutes, this little girl rose up, could talk, and walked with her mother back to the streetcars. Also, in Maria's meetings, many were baptized in the Holy Spirit and received gifts of the Spirit. One woman left Maria's meeting and died outside of her service, causing a commotion. Maria came over to her and spoke about Jesus being the resurrection and invoked the name that is above death. The woman opened her eyes. In a Dallas service, three deaf and mute people all wept and shouted as God opened their ears and gave them voices. Sinners started weeping and making their way to the altars.

Maria made a monumental turning-point statement to a group of ministers:

In the 24th chapter of Matthew, it says this Gospel of the Kingdom shall be preached to all nations as a witness and then shall the end come. Friends, you cannot go out and preach as we used to. I used to preach hellfire, so you could nearly see the fire, and it took effect then, but the call today is for a different ministry, What is needed is not so much the might of preaching, but the demonstration of the Spirit. Sinners are more hard-hearted than they used to be. You can preach hell...yet they will stand and look you calmly in the face; but let them see the mighty power of God manifested and they are convicted.[5]

Maria's prophetic perception of what it will take to see this atheist, paranormal, and fatherless generation turn to God is supremely profound.

The Prophetic and the Persecution

As hard as Pharaoh and Egypt were, it took more than descriptions from Moses; it took *demonstrations* to get them to budge. We can no longer tolerate descriptions without demonstrations; we must operate from the power dimension to kick our persuasiveness into potency.

In St. Louis, Maria opened up a few meetings in a hall. On the first night, only 18 showed up and two people got saved. She could have gotten discouraged, but she was there to break through, not break down. The crowds grew larger every night. There were a number of remarkable healings that impacted the region. Then she had to set up her tent in a rough section of town. People advised Maria to find another place because violent disrupters had cut down tents in the past. Sure enough, these protesting mobsters showed up and set off firecrackers, disrupted worship, and carried weapons with the intent to draw blood. The Christians in attendance looked like a frightened little flock amidst the crazed, drunken mob. Maria turned to a co-worker and declared, "We will never give up, and if they take us out of the tent before we are ready to go, they will take us out dead." She told the crowd to pray and said that the God of Elijah would answer.

At that point, Maria raised her hands and commanded them to listen. She said the Lord had sent her there to do a good work and that she wasn't leaving until the work was done. Then she prophetically decreed that the Lord would strike dead the first one who tried to harm them. In that moment, the power of God fell and the fear of God seized the multitude. The mobsters started sweating and froze as if in a trance. They started putting out their tobacco pipes and took their hats off. Others fell as though dead, and still others stood with their mouths open. After that, the hoodlums respected Maria. Miracles became normal; healings got more astonishing.

Revival Puts the Super on Your Natural

Maria had breakout meetings in challenging cities such as San Francisco, Salt Lake City, Chicago, and others—all accompanied by souls at the altars, miracles in the seats, visitors at the doors, and God's presence in the atmosphere. Maria expected the power of God to be present at every meeting in signs and wonders, and God did not disappoint her. Maria is one of my favorites, because she was a holy supernaturalist, evangelist, and a revivalist all rolled into one!

Maria never took any glory for herself for the healings, but repeatedly stated that it was only through the power of God that the work was done. Maria would say, "Better the world should call us fools, than God." She understood that man will be proven wrong and God will be proven right, because people have a limited view, but God knows the end from the beginning.

Pentecostal leader Robert J. Craig urged ministers to use her as an example. "If the Pentecostal ministry would study her life and count on God, expecting the supernatural to be revealed in each meeting, what a mighty agency ours would be in the hands of God."[6]

Three Reasons Why Walking in God's Power Is Not an Option

Anyone committed to revival in this generation must be a holy supernaturalist at heart. Like Paul, we must realize that our message should not be in sophisticated speech, but in power demonstrations. Pursuing authentic supernatural power should be a core value of all emerging revivalists and end-time believers. There's nothing the devil would like to see more than for us to push the supernatural power realities of God to the fringe while we operate on human abilities.

Rick Joyner writes in *Shadows of Things to Come*:

The ministry that opened the church age will be the one that closes it. Before the end of this age, there will be a movement to return true apostolic ministry to the church…What does this mean? First, it means that Jesus will be in us to do the works that He did when He walked the earth. Second, it means that the church will accurately represent Him to the world, our present world. Our words must become His words, our works His works.[7]

Without power realities, Christianity will lapse into another earthbound philosophy. Framing is everything in modern culture, and God knows how to frame the Gospel; He frames it with the supernatural. This Gospel is not a doctrine or creed; it's the introduction of another realm. Some who have experienced the supernatural power of God have divorced themselves from it. Revival is needed when everything we do is explainable. I have a core value and motto that says, "Let Jesus be our only explanation." C.S. Lewis once said, "Do not attempt to water Christianity down. There must be no pretense that you can have it with the Supernatural left out.

So as far as I can see, Christianity is precisely the one religion from which the miraculous cannot be separated."[8]

Without power realities, this generation's darkness will go unchallenged. People who are trapped in addictions, sexual immoralities, and demonic oppression need the power of God to get free. Without the miraculous, the demonic can operate and legislate. As the current darkness escalates, we must escalate in the power of God. We need the Holy Spirit's reality afresh. The Holy Spirit has been called "the author of every positive revolution in history," "satan's unsolved problem," or "God's secret weapon."

Without power realities, the army of God does not feel emboldened to take the field. There's something about feeling equipped that releases something profound within an individual. Revivals see God take the field in full view, which causes His sons and daughters to also take the field. In Jerusalem, the young believers of the Church had a strategic revival prayer meeting to fight off insecurity, fear, and possible discouragement. Their petition was that God would stretch forth His hand with miracles and give them boldness to speak (see Acts 4:29-31). In Scripture, a dove symbolizes the Holy Spirit, but we mustn't domesticate the dove. We live in extraordinary times where God is releasing more manifestations of supernatural power than in all of history. Revival has to do with the recovery of the purpose for being the representatives of Jesus on Earth. When this occurs, there is a renewed obedience and courage of God's people to make a stand, wherever they may find themselves.

Carlos Annacondia says:

Time after time I repeat to myself, "I have the power of God. I can count on it. He gave it to me. I must put it into practice. Remember this promise is not just for a few anointed, inspired or privileged individuals. The promise is for anyone who believes in Him."

I See Ya!

I first visited Argentina in the early '90s as a part of a miracle crusade evangelistic outreach. I was brought in to speak to the youth and assist in the night meetings. This was only my second mission's trip and I was admittedly "green."

A woman who was born blind walked up to me with a primitive walking stick. I was walking through the crowd and this Argentine blind lady communicated that she believed that God would heal her if I laid hands on her. The problem was, I didn't believe like that and had never been used in a creative miracle. I had faith for runny noses and ringing ears, but that's about it. I looked for someone else to lay hands on her, but everyone else was busy. So I prayed a shaky prayer, beating around the bush of her need. Suddenly, she screamed, "My eyes!" Then she dropped her walking stick and chased me. I was freaked out that this lady had never seen and now had 20/20 vision. When I got back to my campus, I felt so bold and stepped into a greater supernatural walk. We must never allow our hearts to be penetrated by the idea that you and God can't handle the situation before you. It may take some time to see a great manifestation of power, but if we will stand and pray, God will release His purposes.

11

End-Time Ingatherings and the Harvest of Revival

Revival is the fire of God invading the affairs of men so that they see and experience the amplified Presence of God.—Joy Dawson

When revival comes, the rules change. What normally happens goes out the window as the wind of the Spirit fills a region. Revivals bring back to spiritual life believers who appropriate the fullness of the Holy Spirit, resulting in unbelievers being engaged on whole new levels.

Isaiah prophesied of an end-time ingathering as well as a revival:

Arise, shine; for your light has come! And the glory of the Lord is risen upon you. For behold, the darkness shall cover the earth, and deep darkness the people; but the Lord will arise over you, and His glory will be seen upon you. The Gentiles shall come to your light, and kings to the brightness of your rising (Isaiah 60:1-3).

The Gentiles coming to the light speaks of unbelievers coming to Christ. Later on it says the *"abundance of the sea turning to you"* which is describing a great number of souls coming into the Kingdom. This mighty prophetic passage begins with a call to revived believers to get them into position for the Lord to arise over them. Even kings (people of authority and prominence) will be supernaturally drawn to the divine magnetism we will display as we rise in revival with the Gospel message.

The evangelist (especially at the outset of revival) is an office of declaration of the manifested presence of God. Declaring truth is the designated duty of an evangelist; this is the practical expression of manifesting His illumination. We need some apostolic audacity to boldly speak the truth and believe for Heaven to back up the words so the lost will see the One we represent. We must keep a clear sense of missionary purpose and remember the Great Commission.

Jerking and the Prince of Camp Meeting Preachers

From 1750 to 1770, the spirit of revival gradually died out of churches in America. Before the turn of the century, the general state of the Church was one of apathy and coldness. One reason was that France flooded the colonies with books of atheism and anti-faith literature. In Paris, the boast was openly made that in a short while Christianity would be blotted from the earth, and these threatening predictions were echoed in America. In 1793, the Kentucky legislature voted to do away with the services of a chaplain. In many towns, there were no worship services and hundreds of thousands of people were without the Gospel.

Without divine intervention to save God's people, the boast of Paris might have come true. The Revival of 1800 came without any warning signs. Peter Cartwright, an early Methodist circuit rider, was a major player in this revival. Cartwright was born in 1785 to a soldier of the Revolutionary War. His mother was a devout Methodist Christian. He inherited both a great love of liberty and the power of faith. His family moved from Virginia to Kentucky, which positioned him to be thrust into history. He was raised in a rough area called Rogues Harbor, where outlaws and violent fugitives, who defied all law and terrorized other settlers, settled. When the Cartwrights settled in Kentucky, there were murders and other immoral behaviors going on like horse racing, gambling, and alcoholism—and this was just what happened on Sundays.

One evening when Peter Cartwright was 16, he went to a wedding party and spent most of the night dancing. Peter loved card playing and was admittedly a "wild, wicked boy." But he found himself restless after a God-encounter at this party. For three months, he was under deep conviction, fearing that he was seriously lost.

Then the Cane Ridge camp meeting came. Peter was one of 25,000 who attended. Never had so many families camped on grounds, and never had so many people been affected with involuntary physical manifestations. This revival was also instrumental in sparking what became known as the Restoration Movement, which was committed to authentic New Testament Christianity. At these camp meetings, there was off-the-chart excitement as the crowd rushed from preacher to preacher hearing the call to get right with God. Men and women by the hundreds fell to the ground unable to help themselves. These meetings lasted for weeks. It was not unusual for seven preachers to be proclaiming from different stands to thousands at the same time. Thousands would break out shouting, which could be heard from miles away.

It was in this environment that Cartwright had a Damascus Road type of conversion. Peter received a mighty baptism of the Holy Spirit and began to spend large amounts of time on his knees seeking God. Peter didn't have a formal education, but began to preach Christ and took advantage of every situation to bring people to Christ in community after community. He went through storms, snow, and rain, climbed mountains, hiked through valleys, plunged through swamps, yet he never wore out. Keith Hardman, author of the *The Spiritual Awakeners*, wrote, "One reason Cartwright became so well known was his dexterity in handling difficult occasions and disturbances caused by rowdies, which sometimes called for bare fists."[1] Mary Stewart Relfe, author of *Cure of All Ills*, wrote:

> The whole of the frontier—Kentucky, Tennessee Ohio, North and South Carolina and everywhere that Peter traveled experienced Spiritual Awakening! Civic righteousness followed him. Morality and integrity were earmarks of the areas where he labored.[2]

Dancing With the Creator of the Stars

Back when I was in high school, there was a dance club in San Francisco called the Palladium. Imagine one Saturday night an emerging revivalist walking in, getting the DJ to stop mixing, taking the microphone, and announcing that he wanted to invite the presence of the Lord, all of this while holding the hand of a pretty gal. Then in the midst of the prayer, the girl falls on the ground sobbing for God's mercy, the DJ runs away praising God, and people go out in the power. Then, at the end of the night, the Soul Train dancers are saved. This emerging revivalist stays and preaches the next several days, leaving a church in his wake. The sign on the building goes from the Palladium Club to Palladium Christian Center, and holds services for all the people who got saved and more. Sound far-fetched? This happened to Peter Cartwright.

One night while crossing the Cumberland Mountains to go preach, Peter Cartwright chose to stay the night at a lodge. This lodge had a dance going on, and Peter sensed his assignment. This scene was exactly what God had delivered him from, and the Holy Spirit was about to add to that number. Here's how this incident is told in Peter Cartwright's autobiography:

> ...I rode up and asked for quarters, inasmuch as they had party meeting there that night to have a little dance...I quietly took my seat in one corner of the house, and the dance commenced. I sat quietly missing, a total stranger, and greatly desired to preach to this people. Finally, I concluded to spend the next day Sabbath there and to ask the privilege to preach to them. I had hardly settled this point in my mind, when a beautiful ruddy young lady walked very gracefully up to me...and invited me out to take dance with her. I can hardly describe my thoughts or feelings on that occasion. However, in a moment I resolved on in a desperate experiment. I rose as gracefully as I could...The young lady moved to my right side; I grasped her right hand with my right hand...in this position we walked on the floor...The (African-American) man, who was the fiddler, began to put his fiddle in the best order. I then spoke to the fiddler to hold a moment, and added that for several years I had not undertaken any matter of importance without first asking the blessing of God upon it, and I desired now to ask the blessing of God upon this beautiful young lady and the whole company...Here I grasped the young lady's hand tightly, and said, "Let us all kneel down and pray," and then instantly dropped on my knees and commenced praying with all the power of soul and body that I could command.[3]

The young lady tried to get away, but she got rocked by the power of God and hit the floor in conviction. The fiddler ran into the kitchen crying, "What is going on!" People started weeping and many fell to their knees. Peter sang a worship song and prayed as 15 people got saved on the spot. His Holy Ghost meeting lasted a total of three days, with many more getting saved. Peter appointed the landlord as a leader of this new church and sent them a pastor. Peter Cartwright said, "This was the commencement of a great and glorious revival of religion in that region of country and several of the young men converted at this…dance became useful ministers of Jesus Christ."[4]

The Original Modern Mass Revivalist

To understand the revival meteor that George Whitefield became, and how God used him as a human tipping point for an awakening in multiple continents, you must understand the backdrop. In the 18th century, England was shrouded in advancing moral and spiritual darkness. A new face of practical atheism was mean-mugging a generation. Hypocrisy was firmly entrenched in the state churches. Gangs practiced violence all over communities and went on riotous thefts. People began to brew their own liquor, and the nation was obsessed with gin, plunging England into a time called the "Gin Craze."

J.C. Ryle wrote:

England seemed barren of all that is really good. Christianity seemed to lie as one dead. Morality, however much exalted in the pulpits, was thoroughly trampled underfoot in the streets. There was darkness in high places and darkness in low places—a gross thick, religious and moral darkness—a darkness that might be felt.[5]

As England bottomed out, it looks as if the Church was comatose in its own lethargy—the crises were extreme. "Of all the spiritual heroes of a hundred years ago," wrote Ryle, "none saw so soon as Whitefield what the times demanded…"[6] He went on to say, "He preached like a lion. His sermons were life and fire; you must listen whether you like it or not. There was a holy violence about him which firmly took your attention by storm."

Yet Whitefield didn't start off looking like a world changer, at least not a positive one. He was straight thuggish. He regularly stole, lied, gambled, and hung out with the wrong types of people. He got into fights and usually won. He grew up in poverty with a stepfather and mother. Whitefield's real dad died when he was very young. In 1732, at 17, he was sent off to Oxford in order to grow up, but found himself lonely. It was there that the Holy Spirit began to deal with him and he became preoccupied with spiritual things. He read William Law's book, *A Serious Call to a Devout and Holy Life*, and this rocked him. This led to his relationship with John and Charles Wesley and becoming a part of the "Holy Club" at Oxford.

Because Whitefield's zeal was not grace-based, he fasted excessively, which brought about a serious sickness that forced him to leave school in May 1735. He went back home and his zeal caught the attention of the bishop, who ordained George as a deacon. He preached his first sermon in front of his mother and a crowd of others. Some mocked, but most seemed struck. It lasted about 20 minutes, and 15 people became drunk in the Spirit. Some loved it; others blamed him for the disorderly response of these 15.

George was suddenly addicted to sharing the Gospel message. His increasing zeal moved him to witness to people wherever he went. Whitefield stated:

God made me instrumental to awaken several young people who soon formed themselves into a little society and had quickly the honor of being despised at Gloucester as we had been at Oxford.[7]

He started preaching all over, and everywhere he went revivals broke out and sizable harvests came in. He often wept through parts of his message. There were power attestations to his word—many would fall out in the power of the Spirit, shake violently, and sob profusely. When people who mocked Whitefield repeated his messages to entertain tavern customers, people were converted on the spot. At one meeting, a clergyman with a religious spirit once said to George Whitefield, "I'm sorry to see you here." Whitefield replied, "So is the devil." How true was this of this burning revivalist; hell definitely must have feared his appearance!

Finally, he left England for America, with the raging fires of revival in his rearview mirror. The New World voyage was hard, but the soldiers who manned the boat were even harder. By the completion of the trip, many of these guys had been won to the Lord and joined prayer meetings. Georgia was a place of orphanages for the colonists, and George's heart went out to the children. He raised monies and opened schools along the way while winning the lot. He did this in the face of being told, "American colonists were worse than difficult; the place was full of devils." Yet Whitefield saw lasting fruit, traveling up and down the eastern seaboard carrying the Awakening with him.

After some months, George returned to London, thinking that all would be good. But he found the doors of many of the churches were closed to him. So Whitefield began to preach in the open air, which became a pivotal turning point in his ministry. Whitefield started an outdoor campaign at the mouth of a coal mine as the workers got off work. There were 200-plus miners who stood in the field and were eternally impacted. So was Whitefield—open-air preaching released zeal in his soul that caused him to tap into a power flow previously unknown to him. Here he said, "God gives me Heaven upon earth." On a Christmas morning, after spending the whole night in prayer, he said, "God vouchsafed so to fill me with His blessed Spirit that I spoke with supernatural strength, and with as great power as ever I did in my life."[8]

Whitefield loved the prayer meeting and this was his heart's delight. George preached from everywhere but churches, utilizing marketplaces and roofs, ladders, and rocks in fields. Scores were converted and transformed into vessels of righteousness. The next time he went to the coal mines, 2,000 men were waiting to hear him preach. Finally, more than 23,000 people gathered to hear this young evangelist's final sermon. Then he went to Kennington Common, where 30,000 came out and came under conviction, hollering out in repentance.

At this point, anywhere George showed up, huge crowds did also, along with the harvest anointing that impacted the city. There was hardly a town of any significance in England, Scotland, or Wales that he did not visit as an evangelist. The man lived for one thing and that was to preach Christ and reap souls. He preached to an estimated million people, and that was without modern technology. In one gathering near Glasgow, Whitefield spoke to an estimated 100,000 people. Converts totaled 10,000 from that service alone!

The Philly Awakening

George returned to America assured that God wanted a total spiritual revolution of the entire English-speaking world. Whitefield felt strategically led to go to Philadelphia, which was then the largest city in the nation. He had to quickly take his meeting outdoors, as his meetings outgrew any indoor facility and the flames of revival blazed on. Whitefield preached without notes, and it allowed him to uniquely connect with people. Benjamin Franklin spoke of the over-the-top effect Whitefield had on the city:

> It was wonderful to see the change soon made in the manner of our inhabitants. From being thoughtless or indifferent about religion, it seemed as if all the world were growing religious, so that one could not walk through town in an evening without having psalms sung in different families of every street.[9]

Ben Franklin estimated that Whitefield could be heard by 30,000 people without a microphone! Later George Whitefield returned to Philadelphia after rocking New York City, and upon his return thousands sobbed in his meetings. Many were saved, and a city bowed its knee to Jesus. Whitefield was begged by the people not to leave their city. His preaching turned the colonists to the God many had abandoned.

Stephen Mansfield wrote this of Whitefield:

He changed the course of nations, founded institutions that survive to this day, and dug wells of revival that refresh even now. All this was possible because Whitefield believed that to lose one's life for Jesus meant surrendering every moment of the time in which that life is measured.[10]

The bottom line is that this man's open-air preaching was as significant as anything in ushering in the First Great Awakening that certainly altered history and transformed the destinies of untold multitudes.

God's Fire Coming to a Place Near You

I sometimes wonder if the enemy has any sense that a historic rending of the Heavens is about to take place and that long-standing strongholds are about to quake in their boots. I wonder if God also purposely chooses vessels for an awakening that, by divine design, do not look the part of the starting point of a national revival.

Off the west coast of Scotland are a series of islands called the Hebrides. In 1949, a widespread revival hit these islands like a holy tsunami. Some men met in Stornaway and talked about how the churches were abandoned, especially by youth, while worldly places had an audience. At that moment in their barn, an awareness of God seized the atmosphere, and they fell on their faces before God. Then they were caught up in a supernatural stream, which released the realization of revival. This district was about to become an epicenter for a revival earthquake.

Meanwhile, in a small cottage by the roadside in the village of Barvas lived two sisters named Peggy and Christine Smith. (I love their last name.) They were 84 and 82 years old; one was blind and the other doubled over with arthritis. Yet, they fervently contended for revival. On the same night that God's presence touched the seven men in Stornaway, the Spirit visited these two elderly sisters. One of the sisters saw a vision of their church packed out with youth, and she immediately knew that revival was imminent. The Smith sisters believed that the vessel God had chosen for revival was Rev. Duncan Campbell. After an initial hesitancy, Campbell came, only intending to stay for ten days. He ended up staying for three years!

In the initial meeting where Campbell preached, the service was very underwhelming. One of the deacons said, "Don't be discouraged, it is coming. I hear the rumbling of Heaven's chariot wheels."[11] Some of the people, including some youth, went next door and had a prayer meeting. At three o'clock in the morning, the heavens opened and God swept in. When they walked outside, they found people crying out for mercy on their faces out on the country road. Over 100 young people were at a dance and didn't have God in their thoughts when suddenly the power of God fell on them. Duncan Campbell said, "They fled from the hall as a man fleeing from a plague." They went straight to church and saw lights on in the house of God. The next morning, 14 buses came from all over the island for the meetings, while hardened sinners began to confess their sins. About 600 people trying to get to church were hit by the power of God and fell on their knees in front of the police station.

One night, about 20 people were walking at midnight and heard heavenly music and hit the ground, fearing that it was the end of the world. Churches were crowded from morning till the early hours of the following morning. On one occasion, 14 young men were talking about how much beer to bring to a dance on Friday. Suddenly, one of the guys said that something was happening to him and each of them hit their knees for over an hour, were converted, and became ushers in the church.

The fire of revival was so intense that unbelievers were trying to move off the island for fear that they would get converted. Unbelievers were becoming an endangered species. It was said that the worst of sinners, the drunkards, the prostitutes, and the God-haters, were crying out to God to save them. Many of them were literally found lying helpless by the roadside with conviction. The harvest of souls was staggering—it was estimated that 75 percent of the people saved during this revival were converted outside of church and many without anyone witnessing to them.

Heaven's Butterfly Effect Is Awaiting

One of the principles that is driven home in past revivals is how important a vessel's obedient cooperation is to see the winds of God released. In many instances an individual stepped out to believe God and the result was a holy tornado that drew an enormous number of people into the Kingdom and altered nations. In God, small steps carried out by revivalists on the front end of a move of God can gloriously shock the world.

Edward Lorenz was a meteorologist at Massachusetts Institute of Technology who loved the study of weather. He basically found out that a small change in one place can have large effects down the road (the Butterfly Effect). The phrase refers to the idea that a butterfly's wings might create tiny changes in the atmosphere that may ultimately alter the path of a tornado and accelerate or even prevent its occurrence in a certain location. The flapping wing represents a small change in the initial condition of the system, which causes a chain of events leading to large-scale alterations of events. Had the butterfly not flapped its wings, the trajectory of the system might have been vastly different. While the butterfly does not "cause" the tornado in the sense of providing the energy for the tornado, it does "cause" it in the sense that the flap of its wings is an essential part of the initial conditions resulting in the tornado, and without that flap that particular tornado would not have existed. The principle point is key to understanding that what you do from this point on is key to the end-time purposes of the Father for your nation.

Over 200 years ago a spiritual tornado swept through the United States, and this movement became known as the Second Great Awakening. The Second Great Awakening may have impacted the United States more than any other revival. Yet this great move began in June of 1800 in Logan County, Kentucky, by the obedience of a struggling pastor, James McGready, who had moved there from North Carolina. He came to a place nicknamed "Rogue's Harbor," considered satan's stronghold (not exactly the place for a church plant or Bible study)

McGready took over that fledgling small works (which were not exactly hungry for a move of God), including the Red River Meeting House. At first he ministered without great results and felt generally ineffective. He needed greater spiritual influence in this area and greater spiritual leverage against the dark powers holding back the harvest. So he enlisted Christians to covenant to seek God for more. They would pray twice a week for revival and fast once a month for breakthrough. McGready told his people:

> When we consider the word and promises a compassionate God...we find the strongest encouragement for Christians to pray in faith...for the conversion of their fellow-men. None ever went to Christ when on earth, with the case of their friends, that were denied.

His small steps of obedience created changes in the atmosphere that would release a tornado across a greater region than they would realize. Finally in a service in summer of 1800, Logan County, aka satan's stronghold, became ground zero for a revival that saw startling conversions and overflowing zeal among believers. Very shortly, people were coming from a 100-mile radius and spending days camping out just to be in the atmosphere of a bona fide move of God. McGready and his people first saw an atmospheric revival (where people can feel the presence of God) translate into a geographic revival (where the presence of God finds you). History shows that the labors of McGready continued to gain steam and became known as the Second Great Awakening that impacted a nation!

Upgrading Your Spiritual Influence

McGready and the Red River believers covenanted together with a fast along with their cry for revival. Those who are a part of a brand-new breed of revivalists will recognize this holy weaponry of past revivals and employ them to the fullest. Isaiah underscores the significance of a chosen fast in his prophecy:

> *Is this not the fast that I have chosen; to loose the bonds of wickedness, to undo the heavy burdens, to let the oppressed go free, and that you break every yoke? ...Then your light shall break forth like the morning, your healing shall spring forth speedily, and your righteousness shall go before you; the glory of the Lord shall be your rear guard* (Isaiah 58:6,8).

This passage gives us the immediate benefit for combining fasting with our prayers for revival. We are told: 1) your light shall break forth like the morning, and 2) your righteousness shall go before you. These two supernatural effects are the secret to supernatural influence. Prophetic intercessor William Ford III says:

> Influence at its core is about capturing the affections of another. Thoughts, decisions and outcomes are altered and determined as a result. The degree to which a person has ultimately gripped the heart of another will determine the depth of influence that person can exert over the other.

Influence is the key issue and will characterize new school forerunners who are about to come forth. Prophetic forerunners are like signs and living tokens. Their lives are like living stories that communicate not only to their personal lives what the Lord is saying, but also to the Church and world at large by modeling through example.

You are a forerunner generation, and we were given a great example of a forerunner by John the Baptist. John the Baptist (JB) had an undeniable influence that could not be accounted for by external things. In fact, there is no explanation in the natural for his draw. He wasn't giving out Krispy Kreme donuts or Starbucks coffee. He didn't have air conditioned buildings, PowerPoint (though his life pointed pretty powerfully), or comfortable theater seating available. He was a voice crying out in the wilderness. Yet crowds went to see him in droves (see Matt. 3:5-6). No one had a more effective testimony or carried greater influence than John the Baptist in his day (until Jesus). King Herod was afraid that his influence could cause a revolution against his rulership. We are told that JB came for the purpose of being an epic witness of the Light, so he would draw the masses to Christ (see John 1:7). So the question remains how are we going to see a revival harvest and be end-time in-gatherers?

JB had a fasted lifestyle (see Matt. 9:14; 3:4), and this is what connected him to Isaiah's twofold benefit of light breaking forth and righteousness going before him. I wrote in *Prophetic Evangelism*, "It is proven that what we sacrifice and suffer for is what we become most attached to…. The way we live is a reflection of the state of our hearts. Yet the state of our hearts is enflamed by our lifestyles." [12]

This truth consumed JB, and he saw an extreme radical radiation flow from his life that compelled his generation. Light and righteousness are so crucial to our influence in this hour. These two components speak of both intensified influence (light breaking forth) and a super-sized testimony (righteousness going before you). The serious harvest resulting from JB's testimony and his powerful influence upon his generation came from the grace upon his life through his fasted lifestyle. JB had allowed his conviction to sink deeper than his contemporaries, and this brought a greater authority for influence. The deeper your convictions, the stronger your influence, and those will usher many into the Kingdom. The person who influences the thoughts of his or her times influences all the times that follow and has made his or her impression on eternity. Now is the time to bring that influence and your super-sized testimony into the marketplace and affect eternity right where you're at!

12

Chosen to Change the Course of History

When you become a Christian, Jesus will invade your life and make you into somebody He can use to change the world....That was never taught to me when I was growing up. All I was told was that being a Christian meant I would go to Heaven when I died. I was never told that the primary reason Jesus saved me was to...change the world into the kind of world He willed for it to be when He created it.—Tony Campolo

Blockbuster budgets are put into making epic movies that feature an unsung-individual rising up to save the day for the masses. The reason these blockbusters are so engaging is that you were created with a massive mission-op in your spiritual DNA. God Himself is one big pent-up revival waiting to happen, and He created you in His image!

You are original, resourceful, and imaginative, and you are called to express God's breath and life wherever you go. You are part of God's Body, and His Body is His instrument for change in the earth. God will never propose any other stratagem to accomplish what He purposed in the earth.

You are the light of the world and the salt of the earth. God really believes in you. With the Holy Spirit living inside you, and Christ's anointing on you, you are meant to be a sign and token of what the world can step into, namely their destiny as children of God.

The Secret Behind Worldwide Influence

Remember Jonah? Let's look again at his story and see why Jonah was reluctant to go to Nineveh in the first place:

But it displeased Jonah exceedingly, and he became angry. So he prayed to the Lord, and said, "Ah, Lord, was not this what I said when I was still in my country? Therefore I fled previously to Tarshish; for I know that You are a gracious and merciful God, slow to anger and abundant in lovingkindness, One who relents from doing harm" (Jonah 4:1-2).

Jonah knew that God was abundant in lovingkindness and relented from doing harm. This rebellious prophet had an incredibly accurate understanding of the Father's nature, especially in the Old Testament context. Our influence in the earth is largely impacted by what we believe the Father has in His heart to release. Jonah's prejudice almost caused him to miss changing the course of history for a nation. Pre-fish, un-revived Jonah was not awake and alive enough to step into nation-turning influence. Sure, the Ninevites were persistent in their sin, but God is more relentless in unfathomable mercy.

Martin Luther King Jr. was organizing a march when the town authorities told him, "If you do that march, we are going to beat you with clubs and let attack dogs loose on you." He replied,

"After you are done, I am going to love you." King's heart was set on a desired outcome, and he would lower his vision to the alternative. Now God never has been or ever will be soft on sin—it cost Him His Son's sacrifice—but He will not deny who He is in the dimension of rich mercy. Mercy is God's primary attribute:

> *For judgment is without mercy to the one who has shown no mercy. Mercy triumphs over judgment* (James 2:13).

> *But God, who is rich in mercy, because of His great love with which He loved us...* (Ephesians 2:4).

There's no other explanation for why God has sent revival to the places He has throughout history. Revival historian J. Edwin Orr studied the dynamics and characteristics of a region or culture before revival would break out. He looked at multiple outpourings and came up with *five distinguishing features:*

1) Greed with a rapid increase in violent crime.

2) Occult domination. A nation hungry for the supernatural turns to spiritualism.

3) Immorality—a philosophy of "free love" is accepted by many.

4) Commercial and political corruption. Bribes and illegal practices are common.

5) Atheism, apathy, and indifference to God, the Church, and her message.[1]

The bottom line is this: your nation is as deserving as any, because an outpouring of God's Spirit is an act of mercy. Bryn Jones says, "Any student of past revivals knows that, for the most part, they have broken into generations that had largely abandoned God."[2] We qualify. Now we must position ourselves to cooperate with God to see one released. The enemy wants you to feel falsely disqualified—don't help him out!

J. Edwin Orr addressed this:

One finds that the pessimists fulfill their own ideas in themselves (see Proverbs 23:7). As soon as a man starts talking about the impossibility of Revival, his own work is beginning to shrivel up. The man who believes in Revival is the man who sees results.[3]

You could make the case from Jonah's story that Christians are as much to blame for not being revived as sinners are for not being converted. It's funny that Jonah was not surprised by a former wicked nation's national fast, but was disappointed that God showed compassion instead of righteous anger. I sometimes wonder if darkness works as hard to keep the Church doubtful of God's mercy as it does the sinner.

I'm convinced God had decided to extend mercy to the Ninevites before they repented, and this is seen in several ways. First, God didn't send the prophets Amos or Hosea (who were available) because they would have obeyed and not detoured like Jonah. Amos was a shepherd who released the hope of a Savior as well as the prophetic word of an enormous harvest that would spill into the next season (see Amos 9:13). Had God issued the assignment to Amos, he would have had the heart to go immediately. Likewise, Hosea was a prophet of keen awareness and strong loyalty to the Lord. Plus, he had a prostitute wife and would have loved the business trip. Yet, God chose Jonah—rebellious and prejudiced in his heart toward the Ninevites.

Jonah was most likely to defect from this assignment, but God, who knows the end from the beginning, knew what He was getting. In fact, by rebelling, Jonah played right into the purpose and plans of the Father. God wanted to get a "sign" to the Ninevites, and Jonah fit the bill. The Father who writes the life-script of the righteous knew that Jonah's delay would allow for God's surprise to be set. Had he sent those other two prophets, He would have had to judge Nineveh, because Nineveh was too hardened at that point to repent. They needed a sign and some time:

> *Therefore the Lord will wait, that He may be gracious to you; and therefore He will be exalted, that He may have mercy on you. For the Lord is a God of justice; blessed are all those who wait for Him* (Isaiah 30:18).

Biblical scholars tell us that Nineveh worshiped fish. So what did God do but pull his wayward prophet out of the stomach of what they venerated. Jonah's sign is that an element of apparent destruction supernaturally becomes an element of preservation. The pattern is that God cultivates His prophetic purposes in cemetery circumstances, where there is no hope apart from divine intervention. When Jonah was burped up before Nineveh, they witnessed the power of God Almighty, who could pull His messenger out of the belly of their supposedly unrivaled god. The resurrection of dead things is crucial to Christianity!

The genius of our God is in the strategies He has for nation takeovers. One of the most underrated aspects of God is His supreme ability to devise means to get people's attention and then people's hearts:

> *For we will surely die and become like water spilled on the ground, which cannot be gathered up again. Yet God does not take away a life; but He devises means, so that His banished ones are not expelled from Him* (2 Samuel 14:14).

Nineveh's "devised means" had to involve the sign of Jonah.

When Jonah finally spoke to Nineveh, he said, *"Yet forty days and Nineveh shall be overthrown,"* which is very revealing of God's agenda. The first part, *"yet forty days,"* is all about mercy. Why would God give those 40 days if it was already in His heart to destroy Nineveh for their sins? It would have just been a quick "You are judged!" and fiery brimstone would have fallen. Some Christians don't believe that we will see revival because our nation deserves judgment. Frankly, I wouldn't disagree with that statement, but there is a difference between judgment deserved and judgment designated. The secret behind worldwide influence is a deep conviction of the Father's eternal plan to crown His Son's finished sacrifice. The secret is based in the belief that the Kingdom message will have a worldwide impact and the final say in the earth.

Seizing Cultures and Spiritual Atmospheres

A most important discovery is that people live according to the dominant force in their environment. People don't act the way they act for no reason. Certain things are more likely to happen because of a prevailing spiritual atmosphere. Emerging revivalists must understand this concept and know what it takes to seize the spiritual atmosphere and establish a culture, which in turn impacts a region.

A wholehearted agreement to spiritual invitation (revelation or temptation) releases a spiritual *draw* or a spiritual *sway*. A spiritual *draw* is what Heaven releases to an individual and a spiritual *sway* is what hell releases upon an individual:

> *And I, if I am lifted up from the earth, will draw all peoples to Myself." This He said, signifying by what death He would die* (John 12:32-33).

> *We know that we are of God, and the whole world lies under the sway of the wicked one* (1 John 5:19).

The *draw* versus the *sway* plays out in nation after nation. By lifting Jesus up and elevating the light of a transformational lifestyle, you can create a spiritual draw or the makings of the hurricane of revival. A hurricane has a low-pressure center called a vortex that pulls in air so violently that it alters everything in its path. The apostle Paul was a walking vortex in every city he visited.

But a spiritual invitation can also come from darkness that will also cause an influence, which is a spiritual sway. When people give themselves to unrighteousness in a region, it also carries the potential to pull people into its vortex. Yet the *draw* (Heaven's pull) can gain greater spiritual gravitational forces and break people from the power of the *sway* (hell's pull). In other words, light has infinitely more power than darkness.

These two influences can also be described as conviction and seduction. Conviction is what the Holy Spirit uses to draw you to the Father, while seduction is what the enemy uses to sway you to darkness. When conviction or seduction finds agreement, it produces atmosphere. An atmosphere that is sustained and is supported over time establishes a culture. When an atmosphere is stamped authoritatively with total agreement, it brings with it the capacity to draw people to the original purpose agreed upon. For example, somewhere along the line, Mardi Gras' vortex shifted, no longer celebrating a Lenten event but now pulling people into something completely different. People going to Mardi Gras plunged themselves into immoral behavior, which in turn sways others to be captivated by the same immorality. But this could work for righteousness. If we abandon ourselves in agreement to God's activity, causing atmospheres to shift over places, people could come into conviction and God-consciousness.

We need new-breed revivalists who will align themselves with timeless covenants for a revival as well as stamping their regions with a violent agreement that lays hold of the Kingdom.

The Greatest Revival of the Modern Era

As a youngster, Evan Roberts' most consuming passion was revival. He wrote a friend, "For eleven years, I have prayed for a revival. I could sit up all night to read or talk about revivals. It was the Spirit that moved me to think about a revival."[4] At the age of 13, he burned in intercession for revival in Wales.

An evangelist, Seth Joshua, conducted a meeting that Roberts attended. Joshua closed by saying, "Lord, bend us." Those words pierced Evan's heart and he left saying, "Lord, bend me!" At that moment, the Holy Spirit fell on him and he was baptized in the Spirit. Evan started to ask the Father for 100,000 souls and he sensed God all over that prayer. God came upon Roberts so mightily that his bed would often shake. Evan had a vision where he saw a brilliant heavenly body and an arm stretched out to the world, with a piece of paper that said, "100,000." Evan Roberts went to his friend Sidney Evans and told him, "I have a vision of all Wales being lifted up to Heaven. We are going to see the mightiest revival that Wales has ever known." Then Roberts said to Sidney, "Do you believe that God can give us 100,000 souls now?" Within a matter of months, 100,000 souls were converted!

The editor of *The London Methodist Times* went to the revival and this is what he said about it:

> For it is a very real thing, this Revival, a live thing which seems to have a power and a grip which may get hold of a good many of us who at present are mere spectators.

He finished up his interview with a telling statement:

> There is something there from the other world. You cannot say whence it came or whither it is going, but it moves and lives and reaches for you all the time. You see men and women go down in sobbing agony before your eyes as the invisible Hand clutches at their heart. And you shudder. It's pretty grim, I tell you. If you are afraid of strong emotions, you better give the revival a wide berth.[5]

This explanation gives you the sense of the awesomeness of this move. In the awakening in Wales, there were thousands of young, fresh converts filled with the Spirit. Similar to Pentecost, these firebrands plucked from the fire went everywhere preaching the Word.

Effects of the Revival

The resulting wake from the tidal wave of God's blessing was surreal. Crime rates dramatically dropped off, and the alcohol and gambling business went belly-up. One bar owner came out holding a mug of beer inviting a new convert to come have a drink. The new convert, holding up his Bible, replied, "No; we're going with this now. This is the key to Heaven, and that to hell." Judges wore white gloves to signify that there were no cases to go to trial. People who visited the revival went back with holy radioactivity, so that revivals would break out in their home countries.

It was said that during this revival, hardly 15 minutes passed without people praying for the bondage of sin to be broken off of themselves and others. Bookshops sold out of Bibles. Notorious blasphemers were transformed and began quoting Scriptures and testifying in open-air meetings. The Agnostic Society and Infidel Clubs were disbanded because their leaders were converted. The days were filled with services, and these meetings would all be packed with hundreds standing outside. People coming to the revival by train sang and prayed on the way to the station and even in the train all the way there. The revival turned everyone into evangelists and intercessors. Wales became a God-fearing nation again.

It's been reported that over a period of two years, this revival affected almost five million people, making it the greatest revival of the modern era.

Revival Activation and the "Hidden Seed"

Six hundred years ago, there was a man executed for defying the corrupt religious system. He was a reformer named Jan Hus, and he became the first martyr of the Reformation. Hus contended that the Scriptures be translated immediately into native tongues of all people so everyone could receive the Word directly. Corrupt clergy opposed this. Hus began a work among the people of Moravia and taught them the Bible, but the religionists didn't approve. When they eventually realized that nothing would stop Hus, the corrupt religious hierarchy sought to have him burned at the stake. Before Hus was executed, he prophesied that God had put "hidden seed" in the spiritual ground of the Moravians that one day would spring up into revival.

Two hundred years later, John Amos Comenius came on the scene in Moravia. He pastored while religionists came to drive out the Moravian Christians from their homeland and killed many. He led the Moravian Christians out of persecution into neighboring Poland. Comenius never saw his home again and the Moravians were refugees for the next hundred years.

Comenius echoed Hus's word, decreeing that the "hidden seed" would sprout up in a hundred years, activating revival. Refusing to be discouraged, Comenius repeated this prophecy to his listeners up until his death.

A hundred years later, Nikolaus Zinzendorf was born into a wealthy aristocratic family. During his training as a young aristocrat, Zinzendorf visited an art museum in Dusseldorf, where he looked upon a painting of the crucified Christ with the phrase, "This have I done for You—now what will you do for me?" It seemed like Christ spoke those very words to his heart. He vowed that day to abandon his all for Jesus in complete dedication.

At 27, he took in a Moravian refugee. In a short time, he began to disciple 300 Moravians who lived on his estate. One day, Zinzendorf came across Comenius's writings in a library, which contained the prophetic word that Hus' "hidden seed" would resurrect into a righteous revival in a hundred years. When Zinzendorf looked at the date of the prophecy, he noticed that it was exactly a hundred years before. He stepped into this divine moment and changed the course of history.

He called the Moravians together on August 12, 1727, and they prayed all night, launching what is called the "Moravian Pentecost." After a hundred years, the "hidden seed" had been activated and was bringing forth revival just as Comenius had spoken. This ignited a 110-year prayer revival that launched the most significant early missions movement to date. One of the Moravian missionary teams voluntarily sold themselves into slavery so they could spread the Gospel among slaves. Hidden seed is awaiting its activation over your life right now!

Ain't No Mountain High Enough

Over 35 years ago, God gave several men virtually an identical vision for how to advance the Gospel of the Kingdom in this generation, as well as how to reach a nation for God. In 1975, Bill Bright, founder of Campus Crusade for Christ, and Loren Cunningham, founder of Youth with a Mission, had lunch in Colorado. As the story goes, Cunningham and Bright each had a vision given to them by God of seven categories of society in which believers could turn the nations to God. Dr. Lance Wallnau says, "He who occupies these mountains controls the harvest."

Cunningham and Bright were both given the names of the seven mountains: media, government, education, economy, religion, arts and entertainment, and family.

The mountain of *religion* is very pivotal. Spiritual beliefs impact the behavior of masses. Kingdom people recognize how God's truth plays into the eternal scheme of things. Yet, this mountain carries huge ramifications in this realm of time and space. Countries veiled with idolatry and false religion play into satan's plan to keep populations in bondage. Truth sets people free, and the Spirit of the Lord brings liberty. The Spirit is setting apart people who will rise up in their callings to bring a new clarity in vision, mobilizing to pioneer new works.

The mountain of *government* is also crucial in influencing people for obvious reasons. God gave government to provide freedoms and boundaries. When governments are corrupt and unjust laws prevail, it brings a dark oppression on the populace of a nation and disgrace (anti-grace):

> *When the righteous are in authority, the people rejoice; but when a wicked man rules, the people groan* (Proverbs 29:2).

We need a fresh generation of Spirit-directed believers to step into the political and governmental arenas. I believe that God is placing this mantle on more individuals specifically for end-time purposes.

The mountain of *economy* also includes business, technology, and science. People who carry influence in this sphere create economic worlds in which people must function. It is also obvious that greed and poverty can negatively affect someone's opportunities. As wealth changes hands, so do options, influence, and connections. I have seen God give His people wisdom, inventions, and ingenuity to produce wealth, which in turn allows ministries and nations to receive godly benevolence.

The mountain of *family* is ultimately crucial due to the fact that this will impact the heart of an individual and open or close him or her to other influences. The enemy knows this and attempts to break apart this God-ordained structure with assaults. The issue of the stability of a man and woman in covenantal agreement, who train offspring to honor, is far reaching. Discord and divorce affect the very Earth. Like Noah, who saw to it that his family made it to the ark, we must prioritize our family. The issues of purity, morality, and fidelity must be fostered in us and in the generation to follow.

The mountain of *arts and entertainment* has grown in modern culture to unforeseeable proportions. It includes sports, fashion, music, and other facets of celebration in modern culture. If you think of how much time, effort, and money are spent each year in this sphere, you realize its importance today. Celebrities in the film or music industries have become today's preachers. Movies are sermons put to film, and songs are sermons put to melodies. The arts and fashion industry impacts people in terms of the power of what's suggested or endorsed. I'm excited to see revivalists getting a burden to go into these industries with the heart to bring light. We seemed to have turned a corner and seen a prophetic voice raised up, but we need many more.

The mountain of *education* is another mountain that is highly contested. Years ago, education reflected a belief in the uniqueness of humanity and God's divine purpose for humanity and the meaning of life. Now educators remove faith in God from the equation. Evolution has displaced creationism and the Creator's demand upon our lives. Most teachers push an agenda that embraces secular humanism and unbiblical views of family. Daily, values are communicated in the classroom that are contrary to the fear of the Lord. I thank God for the many righteous people who feel called to go into the field of education.

The mountain of *media* refers to print and broadcast news and Internet channels. The term "putting a spin" on a story has become a serious fixture in media today. We see so much information that people use to direct their lives today in newspapers, networks, the Internet, magazines, and radio broadcasts. Media can get officials elected because a report dictates outcomes and attempts to discredit Christians. Values and images are constantly driven home through media. I expect to see so many more "marketplace evangelists" rising up to take this mountain for God's glory.

The bottom line is that Christians must demonstrate God in every sphere of society, not just behind church walls. I'm convinced that there will be a great awakening in the market-place. God has not made the distinction between sacred and secular that we have made. He told us: *"Let your light so shine before men…"* (Matt. 5:15). In order to do this, God's army needs to infiltrate all spheres of society where men are. The Lord has called each of us to excellence, wherever He places us.

It's Personal Now; I'm Taking That Mountain!

Oscar Wilde is quoted as saying, "An idea that isn't dangerous is hardly worth calling an idea at all." If that is the case, Caleb had a big-time idea! Hebron was a mountain territory that Caleb had been waiting on over half his life. God had promised it to his people as an inheritance, but 45 years earlier they were scared out of securing it by the dreaded Anakim:

> *"Now therefore, give me this mountain of which the Lord spoke in that day; for you heard in that day how the Anakim were there, and that the cities were great and fortified. It may be that the Lord will be with me, and I shall be able to drive them out as the Lord said." And Joshua blessed him, and gave Hebron to Caleb the son of Jephunneh as an inheritance. Hebron therefore became the inheritance of Caleb the son of Jephunneh the Kenizzite to this day, because he wholly followed the Lord God of Israel* (Joshua 14:12-14).

Caleb made one of the most astonishing requests in all of Scripture, considering the circumstances. He could have settled in the valley and rode his golf cart around Kadesh Barnea's leisure world. The Anakim were said to be 11 feet tall! Here was an 85-year old, five-and-a-half-foot man ready to beat down an army of 11-foot warriors. Caleb didn't even ask for an army; he just asked for permission to slap an eviction notice on their behinds. Some believers are too easily content with "near enough" moments instead of mountain-taking action. Scholars believed that

Caleb could see this mountain from his wanderings. He had to be thinking, "One day, if I ever get another chance, nothing will stop me from occupying that mountain." This is the Caleb distinction, which every modern-day revivalist must possess.

The Caleb Distinction Characteristics

Calebs are remarkably lionhearted. The Caleb distinction is evidenced within the heart that burns to break into new territories. These revivalists understand that God is calling them to shatter barriers between them and the fulfillment of their destinies. Caleb could have lived off the fact that he stood at an earlier time (see Num. 13:30), but he realized that his victories couldn't be too far removed from his current experience. I'm convinced there is a victory that grows out of a spirit of confidence. Caleb represents revivalists who must move past hearing about their promise to activating the promise of mountain-taking.

Revivalists with the Caleb Distinction refuse to allow the enemy to leave "dark legacies" on their watch. Like the Captain of our salvation, modern-day male and female Calebs realize that destroying dark designs is a major part of our purpose (see 1 John 3:8). Caleb wanted to go to the exact place that had scared the spies. He couldn't allow the lingering memory of God or His people to be of Israel backing off from Mount Hebron. This divine outrage was followed by a super desire for God to answer the challenges of darkness.

Revivalists with the Caleb Distinction expect God moments right where they are. You must expect impartation and breakthrough wherever you show up. A Caleb spirit sees the reality of what God has promised. One time, Bob Hartley, a prophetic vessel, said to me, "Sean, sometimes you can see more with your eyes closed than you can with your eyes open." Caleb probably closed his eyes several times in the desert, dreaming about taking the mountain back from the Anakim. The Holy Spirit comes to show you what you can attain beyond all you have ever reached before. When a revivalist gets this download, it causes inspiration to hit your life in any situation. It's time to inherit and occupy some mountains.

Changing Impossibilities Into Revival Realities

Roman playwright Plautus once said, "A bell doesn't ring on its own. If someone doesn't pull or push it, it will remain silent." Modern America and the nations of the world need their bell rung. The challenge for every emerging revivalist is how to become a catalyst for a new outpouring and a new sound in the human heart. We have a generation today that does not possess a rallying call or battle cry. They haven't found a cause upon which to leverage their lives. God knows that you are made out of the stuff that desires to give its all to something or someone.

This is the profile on Judge Barak in the Bible, who represents us:

Now Deborah, a prophetess, the wife of Lapidoth, was judging Israel at that time. And she would sit under the palm tree of Deborah between Ramah and Bethel in the mountains of Ephraim. And the children of Israel came up to her for judgment. Then she sent and called for Barak the son of Abinoam from Kedesh in Naphtali, and said to him, "Has not the Lord God of Israel commanded, 'Go and deploy troops at Mount Tabor; take with you ten thousand men of the sons of Naphtali and of the sons of Zebulun; and against you I will deploy Sisera, the commander of Jabin's army, with his chariots and his multitude at the River Kishon; and I will deliver him into your hand.'?"

And Barak said to her, "If you will go with me, then I will go; but if you will not go with me, I will not go!"

So she said, "I will surely go with you; nevertheless there will be no glory for you in the journey you are taking, for the Lord will sell Sisera into the hand of a woman." Then Deborah arose and went with Barak to Kedesh (Judges 4:4-9).

The Book of Judges is a picture of the spiritual history of God's people and their nation's regrettable pattern. After revivals, generations arise who don't know the work that the Lord has done (see Judges 2:7-10). God would raise up a judge and deliver the people. They would in turn honor God, prosper, and defeat their enemies. After a while they would get lax and compromised to the point that it made them vulnerable to their enemies and they would move from the peak of victory to the valley of oppression.

Deborah, a judge, gave this report of the current conditions of the land:

In the days of Shamgar, son of Anath, in the days of Jael, the highways were deserted, and the travelers walked along the byways. Village life ceased, it ceased in Israel, until I, Deborah, arose, arose a mother in Israel. They chose new gods; then there was war in the gates; not a shield or spear was seen among forty thousand in Israel (Judges 5:6-8).

If you could combine CNN and local news reports, you would have a statement of current events similar to this passage of Scripture. The people of God were severely outnumbered and terrorized by the Canaanite army with 900 iron chariots. The enemy had made sudden inroads for the purpose of plundering the people of God into cowardice. As a result, God's people left the mainstream of society. By default, they had gone from a revival mentality to a survival mentality. Because the Israelites were hiding out, they had also abandoned all cultivation and were not trying to build for the future. Today darkness has fully utilized a politically correct spirit and a tyrannical "intolerance" label used to bully folks into withdrawal. Meanwhile, the media aims a blaming pointed finger at the righteous.

When this passage says, *"...there was war in the gates,"* it is speaking of the gates of a city where the leadership met and justice was dispensed. We live in a day where there is a serious shortage of real leaders—leaders who don't take their direction from the mistaken, but get their due north from on high. As a result, justice gets perverted, and injustice is so common that it is expected and renamed to soften the blow.

This was a deliberate attempt by the Canaanites to break the spirit of Barak and his nation. This would lead to hopelessness and futility. Futility says, "It doesn't matter what I do or say, it's not going to change the outcome." In this demonic downsizing of God's people, darkness takes the lead in leadership. The passage also says, *"...they chose new gods."* This is the product of being so blinded to the present expression of God. The adoption of secular humanism as this nation's official religion is highly chronicled. We take in all stray beliefs, sit at a smorgasbord of eastern religions, and wonder why we're hauntingly empty at the end of it.

Jabin was the king of the Canaanites. He fortified cities, and a Philistine named Sisera commanded his army. The Philistines had a monopoly on making weapons and iron. Not only did the Israelites have no weapons, but no one dared to attempt to make them because they had been resisted for 20 years. An impossible situation faced Barak because he faced an army that knew how to be an army. They had the numbers, the artillery, the experience, the recent history, and the psychological advantage. Barak could have thought, "We don't have an army. We don't have any weapons, and they won't let us have any. We don't have any experience; in fact, we've never even tasted victory in my generation. We're not even sure that we want to try."

Overwhelming circumstances are not the measure of a situation. God is able to step into a situation nobody could win and claim a victory with style. To say something is impossible is to say that it is hopelessly difficult and inconceivable. To a true child of God, who is walking out the purpose of God, nothing is impossible.

"Impossible is nothing." Adidas has adopted this slogan, yet it was heavyweight Muhammad Ali who said:

> Impossible is just a big word thrown around by small men who find it easier to live the world they've been given than to explore the power then have to change it. Impossible is not a fact. It's an opinion. Impossible is not a declaration. It's a dare. Impossible is potential. Impossible is temporary. Impossible is nothing.[6]

What does it take to transform an impossible situation into one of life and possibilities? Two things come to mind. The first is what you see all over the Book of Judges before every spiritual upswing, and that is a cry to God. A cry to God is what it takes to make possible the impossible. There are at least five seasons of revival recorded in the book of Judges. The phrase, *"the children of Israel cried unto the Lord"* occurs in connection with each of them. We must want deliverance, not just relief. Then God will raise up revivalists to enact His strategy of awakening. The question is, will you let the symptoms of where we are as a nation move you to the appropriate action?

I Know That You Have Heard Him

Deborah called Barak out and told him that God had chosen him to mobilize an army for a revival of true faith by overthrowing the Canaanites. It's interesting that when a leader of a movement was needed, God went to Naphtali, the scene of the deepest oppression. Naphtali was not only Barak's hometown, but the place of the Canaanite capital. Another thing that stands out is the spiritual influence of Deborah. She chose Barak out of 10,000 men and urged him to raise a standard. Every human being has influence. The Almighty holds you and me accountable for the ways we affect the souls of others. Another thing that stands out is Deborah's question, *"Has not the Lord God of Israel commanded, 'Go and deploy troops…'?"* This suggests that God had previous dealings with Barak.

Many times, when God starts a move, He begins with a word, a dream, or a vision to His chosen vessels, which often catches them off guard. This is important because God controls the unfolding of history through the unwavering certainty of His Word. Then God scripts the steps of individuals who are committed to Him. A revivalist recognizes these truths and implements them with laser-like focus to stir those around them. Deborah's revivalist ministry inspired and mobilized a passive people to awakened, revitalized, activated faith.

Barak responded with some hesitating faith, saying that he would only go if she went with him. Deborah said she would accompany him but said that the victory over Sisera would be credited to a woman! Some other woman, who didn't know she was going to play a part in this prophecy, would get the victory. I would have loved to hear Deborah's prophetic exhortation to Barak on their walk to the battle. God put Deborah the prophetess in place before Barak's mission and exploit. God brought the prophetic movement into place before this unprecedented calling of emerging revivalists. The revealed word of the Lord and prophetic visions will hold the hand of a generation to contend for this upcoming, historic breakthrough.

As history tells us, Sisera caught word that Barak and his men were coming, so Sisera gathered the 900 chariots to the river Kishon. God allowed the "information leak" to draw Sisera out. Deborah described the bizarre phenomenon that happened next. She says the stars fought from Heaven against Sisera (see Judges 5:19-22).

What would neutralize 900 iron chariots against a group of ragtag pedestrians in a valley? That's right—mud, and lots of it. An unexplainable perfect storm came in a blistering fashion against the Canaanites. Their chariots got stuck and their horses fell and the river Kishon overflowed, making them sitting ducks for Barak. Until Israel could take their swords, Barak had to descend upon the enemy with rocks and sticks like the Ewoks attacked the Imperial troops in Star Wars. Sisera ran into a neutral tent trying to escape, but actually ran to his demise. Jael, the woman that Deborah prophesied about, covered Sisera with a blanket, and in epic fashion took him out with a tent peg.

Revivals happen because the stars still fight from Heaven to overwhelm darkness. God still sends a spiritual rain over regions and nations. Heaven continues to select Earth's most unlikely heroes as radical revivalists to break into nations.

An Appeal for an Awakening

God is in this hour looking for people who will occupy a new or forgotten place in the Spirit, revival forerunners who are not afraid to lock horns with the demons of modern culture or religious spirits to create space for a God-invasion. What it all boils down to is this: Are you OK with the spiritual condition of your city, school, workplace, or neighborhood? Are you OK with your spiritual condition? How do you feel when you hear about the great revival experience of those that have gone before you? Martyn Lloyd-Jones rightfully says, "If anything shows our need for revival at the present time it is what we see when we look around us." What do you see? There is no doubt that we are seeing stuff today that was formerly prophesied about. The endtimes are unfolding right before our eyes. Anyone cross-referencing the five o'clock news with the Book of Revelation and prophetic writings can see that something apocalyptic is brewing up right now. Currently a generation is being raised up to violently move Heaven and Earth and lead a spiritual revolution. There is so much at stake, yet the Father has ordained your role in the upcoming Great Awakening and the greatest ingathering to hit the planet ever.

Then Deborah said to Barak, "Up! For this is the day in which the Lord has delivered Sisera into your hand. Has not the Lord gone out before you?" So Barak went down from Mount Tabor with ten thousand men following him. And the Lord routed Sisera and all his chariots and all his army with the edge of the sword before Barak; and Sisera alighted from his chariot and fled away on foot (Judges 4:14-15).

Like the Prophetess

Deborah's word to Barak was, "I've written this book because I believe *you* are the *one!* The question is no longer whether or not revival is coming, but rather *when* and through *whom.* And your answer must be 'Now and through *me.*'" Have you not sensed the Spirit nudging you on to something more? Have you not felt that it is time to embrace a God-sized vision for Heaven's invasion in your world?

That which is spiritually developing right now (signs of revival) are what I dreamt about when I was given visions of coliseums full of people getting saved, healed, and ignited for the glory of God. These open visions are what caused me to lay down my degree and pursue a unique call to run with a generation of fullness of God in a massive outpouring. I recently tweeted (to my son) that a father's desire for a son is to reproduce himself in order that a pattern may not be lost to the world. But then I followed it up with a, "Yet you will take it further and go over the top."

That's exactly why I've given my life to this thing (revival) and have labored on this work (*I Am Your Sign*), because this is also true of you. It's written all over you. You have been sovereignly chosen. This whole journey that I've been on and what I've envisioned about for years (massive awakening) is what we are about to step into. There is a mandate on your life for this; all your dealings have prepared you for this. We are about to step into stadiums being filled, campuses being rocked (for righteousness), and cities being taken. I see it (the reality of your purpose for epic revival) in your eyes every time I've recently stepped into a meeting. I've felt it in your worship as you've sung and heard it in your cries for more of God. It is evidenced in your DNA that demands social justice and in your behavior that declares that it's not OK to be silent in the face of oppression and persecution. You are being raised up as a sign of Heaven's intention in your generation.

God is ready to unveil a radical new mercy in our day that will cause long-standing oppressions to give way and injustices to be terminated as a groundswell of radical new breed revivalists move from the background to the forefront. God is hearing the cries of oppression just like in Moses' day, and Heaven is releasing awakened deliverers who will be in sync with the Spirit of God, walking in the miraculous and moving in Christ's compassion. Not only will they see signs and wonders, but they will also be signs and wonders, and a generation will have to sit up and take notice.

Now let me speak over you. It's our destiny to reap this massive harvest. You were placed in this generation to reap a harvest, the likes of which the world has not seen. You were created for the last-days outpouring and a new signs-and-wonders movement. It is the invoice of our lives to walk in an unusual anointing that is similar to the Book of Acts, only greater. The lame are supposed to walk, the blind to see, and the dead to be raised before you. This is our destiny and preordained life script to unleash the extraordinary, while seeing a divine visitation manifest. The anointing coming to you now is for a Heaven-rendering, history-making, national awakening that will crown the Son with the praises of freshly delivered adoring sons and daughters. Rise up, emerging revivalists, this is your hour. You are their sign!

Endnotes

Introduction

1. G.J. Morgan, *Cataracts of Revival* (Grand Rapids, MI: Zondervan Publishing House), 9-10.

2. Mary Stewart Relfe, *Cure of All Ills* (Prattville, AL: League of Prayer, 1988), 7.

3. Selwyn Hughes, *Why Revival Waits* (Nashville, TN: Broadman & Holman Publishers, 2003), 19.

4. Norman Grubb, *Continuous Revival* (Fort Washington, PA: CLC Publications, 1952), 10.

Chapter 1

1. http://www.jesus.org.uk/ja/mag_revivalfires_murray.shtml.

2. http://www.eaec.org/faithhallfame/dlmoody.htm.

3. Mike Bickle, "A New Expression of Christianity To Cry Out With Prayer and Fasting," Passion for Jesus Ministries, July 18, 2008, http://www.passionforjesus.org/

ANewExpressionofChristianityToCryOutwithPrayerAnd Fasting.html (accessed May 26, 2011).

4. Duncan Campbell, The Price and Power of Revival (n.p.: The Faith Mission, n.d.), 7.

5. Rev. W.F.P. Nobel, A Century of Gospel Work (Philadelphia, PA: C.H. Watts & Co., 1876).

6. http://sentinellenehemie.free.fr/wallisarthur_gb.html.

7. Arthur Wallis, In the Day of Thy Power (Columbia, MO: Christian Literature Crusade, 1956), 47.

Chapter 2

1. Arthur Wallis, *In the Day of Thy Power* (Columbia, MO: Christian Literature Crusade, 1956), 75.

2. Orr, J. Edwin. *The Church Must First Repent*, (Grand Rapids, MI: Zondervan, 1937), 140-142.

3. Bill Johnson, *The Supernatural Power of a Transformed Mind: Access to a Life of Miracles* (Shippensburg, PA: Destiny Image, 2005), 44.

4. Norman Grubb, *The Spirit of Revival* (Scotland, UK: *Christian Focus Publications*) 2003.

5. Ibid.

6. Ibid.

7. Ibid., 27.

8. Ibid., 73.

9. http://www.jesus.org.uk/ja/mag_revivalfires_congo.shtml.

10. Jonathan Edwards, *Thoughts on the Revival in New England,* http://www.ccel.org/ccel/edwards/works1.ix.html .

11. Winkie Pratney, *Revival* (Lafayette, LA: Huntington House Publishers, 1994), 88.

12. Keith Hardman, ,*The Spiritual Awakeners* (Chicago: Moody Press, 1983), 21.

13. Ibid.

14. C.H. Spurgeon, Twelve Revival Sermons (London: Passmore and Alabaster, 1855), 15-16.

15. Keith Hardman, Keith, The Spiritual Awakeners (Chicago: Moody Press, 1983), 2.

16. James A. Stewart, Opened Windows (Asheville, NC: Revival Literature, 1999), 30.

Chapter 3

1. Malcolm Gladwell, *The Tipping Point* (New York: Little, Brown and Company, 2002), 12.

2. Ibid., 19.

3. "The Revival Begins…," 312 Azusa Street, http://www. azusastreet.org/revivalbegins.htm (accessed May 26, 2011).

4. Cecil Robeck, The Azusa Street Mission & Revival (Nashville, TN: Thomas Nelson, 2006), 187.

5. R.E. Davies, I Will Pour Out My Spirit (Tunbridge Wells, England: Monarch Publications, 1992), 223.

6. James Stewart, Opened Windows (Asheville, NC: Revival Literature, 1958).

7. Richard Lovelace, Dynamics of Spiritual Life (Downers Grove, IL: Intervarsity Press, 1979), 131.

8. Selwyn Hughes, Why Revival Waits (Nashville, TN: Broadman & Holman Publishers, 2003), 14-15.

9. A. W. Tozer, The Pursuit of God, http://www.worldinvisible. com/library/tozer/5f00.0888/5f00.0888.03.htm.

10. Brian Edwards, Revival! A People Saturated with God (Carlisle, PA: Evangelical Press, 1990), 50.

11. J. C. Ryle, Christian Leaders of the 18th Century (Carlisle, PA: Banner of Truth, 1978).

12. Richard Riss, A Survey of 20th Century Movements in North America (Baltimore, MD: Peabody, 1988).

13. Ian Malins, Prepare the Way for Revival (Grand Rapids, MI: Chosen Books, 2004).

14. Jonathan Goforth, By My Spirit (Basingstoke, Hampshire, UK: Marshall, Morgan & Scott, 1929), 185.

Chapter 4

1. G.J. Morgan, *Cataracts of Revival* (Grand Rapids, MI: Zondervan, 1952), 21.

2. Wesley Duewel, *Revival Fire* (Grand Rapids, MI: Zondervan, 1995), 352.

3. http://www.prophecynewswatch.com/2011/January12/1286.html.

4. Brian Edwards, *Revival! A People Saturated with God* (Carlisle, PA: Evangelical Press, 1990), 48.

5. Mario Murillo, *Critical Mass* (Port Bolivar, TX: Anthony Douglas Publishing, 1985), 13-14.

6. Brother Andrew, *Unlock Your Hidden Prayer Power* (Santa Ana, CA: Open Doors, 1987).

7. Alvin Reid, *ROAR: The Deafening Thunder of Spiritual Awakening*, 2010. http://alvinreid.com/wp-content/uploads/roar.pdf.

8. Ian Murray, *The Puritan Hope* (Carlisle, PA: Banner of Truth, 1971), 3.

9. Ibid.

10. Ibid., 182-83.

11. Ibid., 258.

Chapter 5

1. Matthew Backholder, *Understanding Revival* (Engelwood, CO: Faith Media, 2009), 38.

2. Ethel May Baldwin and David V. Benson, *Henrietta Mears and How She Did It!* (Delight, AR: Gospel Light Publication, 1966), 232.

3. Richard Riss, *Latter Rain* (Mississauga, ON: Honeycomb Visual Productions, 1987), 30.

4. Carl Brumbuck, *Suddenly...From Heaven* (Spring- field, MO: Gospel Publishing House), 331.

5. Corey Russell, *Pursuit of the Holy* (Kansas City, MO: Forerunner Books, 2006), 24.

Chapter 6

1. http://www.thetravelingteam.org/?q=node/117.

2. D.W. McWilliams, *"A Reminiscence,"* *The Student Volunteer Movement After 25 Years*, 70-71.

3. Jonathon Edwards, *The Great Awakening* Digital History, 1743, www.digitalhistory.uh.edu.

4. John Mott, www.onmovements.com and www.onleadingwell.com.

5. http://www.infoplease.com/us/supreme-court/cases/ar10.html.

6. Arthur Blessitt, *Life's Greatest Trip* (Waco, TX: Word Books, 1970), 26.

7. Ibid.

8. The First Jesus Freak, "A pot-smokin', LSD-droppin' seeker turned Calvary Chapel into a household name. So why is Lonnie Frisbee missing from church history?" *Orange County Weekly*, Mar. 4-10, 2005.

9. "The New Rebel Cry," *Time Magazine,* June 21, 1971, 43.

10. Ernest Baker, *Revivals in the Bible* (The Revival Library, public domain, 1906).

11. Garth M. Rosell and Richard Dupuis, *The Original Memoirs of Charles G. Finney* (Grand Rapids, MI: Zondervan, 1989), 82.

Chapter 7

1. Ian Malins, *Prepare the Way for Revival* (Grand Rapids, MI: Chosen Books, 2004), 115.

2. Winkie Pratney, *Revival* (Lafayette, LA: Huntington House Publishers, 1994), 93.

3. Daniel R. Jennings tells the story in *The Supernatural Occurrences of Charles Finney* (Sean Multimedia, 2009), 35.

4. Arthur Wallis, *In a Day of Thy Power* (Columbia, MO: CityHill Publishing, 1956).

5. Andrée Seu, "Beyond Human Control" *World Magazine*, vol, 23 No. 15 (Jul 26 2008).

6. James Stewart, *Opened Windows* (Asheville, NC: Marshall, Morgan & Scott, 1958), 35, 89.

7. Leonard Ravenhill, *Revival, God's Way* (Bloom-ington, MN: Bethany House, 1986).

8. Jonathan Goforth, *By My Spirit* (Nappanee, IN: Evangel Publishing House, 1983), 20.

9. Eugene Myers Harrison, *The Holy Spirit's Man in China,* http://www.holytrinitynewrochelle.org/your ti18778.html.

10. Wesley Duewel, *Revival Fire* (Grand Rapids, MI: Zondervan, 1995), 270.

11. Jonathan Goforth, *By My Spirit* (Nappanee, IN: Evangel Publishing House, 1983), 131.

12. Ian Paisley, *The Fifty-Nine Revival* (Belfast, Ireland: The Free Presbyterian Church of Ulster, 1958), 39.

13. William J. Harding, *The Ulster Revival of 1859*, http://www.revival-library.org/catalogues/1857ff/harding.html.

14. Ibid.

Chapter 8

1. A.W. Tozer, *Rut, Rot or Revival* (Camp Hill, PA: Christian Publications, 1992), 5.

2. Robert E. Coleman, *One Divine Moment* (Old Tappen, NJ: Fleming H. Revell Company, 1970), 27.

3. J. Edwin Orr, *Prayer and Revival*, http://www.jedwinorr.com/prayer_revival.htm.

4. Fred W. Hoffman, *Revival Times in America* (Boston, MA: W. A. Wilde Company, 1956), 108-9.

5. William Arthur, The Tongue of Fire: Or the True Power of Christianity (London: Hamilton, Adams, and Co., 1856), 363, http://books.google.com/books?id=RfwCAAAAQA AJ&pg=PA363&dq=crown+this+nineteenth+century+wit h+a+revival+of+pure+and+undefiled+religion,+greater+t han+any+demonstration+of+the+Spirit+ever+vouchsafed +to+man&cd=3#v=onepage&q=crown&f=false (accessed May 27, 2011).

6. Ernest Baker, The Revivals of the Bible, The Revival Library, public domain, http://www.revival-library.org/catalogues/genhistory/baker.html.

Chapter 9

1. Wesley Duewel, *Revival Fire* (New York: Harper Collins Publishers, 1995).

2. Charles E. Hambrick-Stowe, *Charles Finney and the Spirit of American Evangelism* (Grand Rapids, MI: Eerdmans, 1996), 110, 113.

3. Mark Shaw, *Global Awakening* (Downers Grove, IL: Inter-Varsity Press, 2010).

Chapter 10

1. Ron Hutchcraft, *Called to Greatness* (Chicago: Moody Press, 2001).

2. James A. Stewart, *Opened Windows* (Asheville, NC: Marshall, Morgan & Scott, 1958), 73,75.

3. G.J. Morgan, *Cataracts of Revival* (Grand Rapids, MI: Zondervan, 1939), 16.

4. Warren Wiersbe, *50 People Every Christian Should Know* (Grand Rapids, MI: Baker Books, 2009), 57.

5. Maria Woodworth-Etter, *Marvels and Miracles* (Bishop's Waltham, Hants, UK: The Revival Library, King's Christian Centre, 1922).

6. Wayne Warner, *For Such A Time As This- Maria, Woodsworth-Etter* (Gainesville, FL: Bridge-Logos, 2004), 218.

7. Rick Joyner, *Shadows of Things to Come* (Nashville, TN: Thomas Nelson Publishing, 2001), 209.

8. C.S. Lewis, God in the Dock (Trustees of the Estate of C.S. Lewis, 1970), 99.

Chapter 11

1. Keith Hardman, *The Spiritual Awakeners* (Chicago: Moody Press, 1983), 144.

2. Mary Stewart Relfe, *Cure Of All Ills* (Prattville, AL: League of Prayer, 1988), 126.

3. Peter Cartwright, ed. W. P. Strickland, *Autobiography of Peter Cartwright, The Backwoods Preacher* (New York: Carlton & Porter, 1856), 86.

4. J.C. Ryle, *Christian Leaders of the Last Century* (London: T. Nelson and Sons, 1869), 153.

5. Ibid.

6. Ibid.

7. A.S. Billingsley, *Life of George Whitefield* (Phila-delphia, PA: PW Ziegler and Co., 1889).

8. George Whitefield, *George Whitefield's Journals, Edinburgh Scotland* (Carlisle, PA: The Banner of Truth trust, 1905), 25.

9. Stephen Mansfield, *Forgotten Founding Father, The Heroic Legacy of George Whitefield* (Nashville, TN: Highland Books, 2001), 133.

10. Stephen Mansfield, Forgotten Founding Father: The Heroic Legacy of George Whitefield (Nashville, TN: Highland Books, 2001), 133.

11. Kathie Walters, Bright and Shining Revival (Macon, GA: Good News Fellowship Ministries), 8.

12. Sean Smith, Prophetic Evangelism (Shippensburg, PA: Destiny Image Publishers, 2004), 56.

Chapter 12

1. J. Edwin Orr, *The Fervent Prayer* (Chicago: Moody Press, 1974).

2. Bryn Jones, "Suddenly, All Heaven Broke Loose!" http://www.therestorer.net/rsudd.html,

3. J. Edwin Orr, *All Your Need* (London: Marshal, Morgan & Scott, 1936), 123.

4. Keith Malcomson, *Pentecostal Pioneers* (Long- wood, FL: Xulon Press, 2008).

5. S.B. Shaw, *The Great Revival in Wales*, 1905. Revival Library, public domain http://www.revival-library.org/catalogues/1904ff/shaw.html.

6. http://www.goodreads.com/author/quotes/46261.Muhammad_Ali.

About Sean Smith

Sean Smith's roots are in the San Francisco Bay Area, where he grew up in the inner city of Oakland. Amidst family tragedy, which included the untimely murder of his father, Sean found his life reeling with pain, but his testimony includes the phenomenal intervention of God.

Sean has spent approximately 25 years in full-time ministry, 10 of which was spent directing campus outreach ministries at the University of the Pacific and California State University, Chico Campuses.

Sean has now been launched into full-time evangelism, conducting outreaches and crusades all over the States and overseas. Sean's messages are prophetic, challenging people to fulfill their destiny in Christ. Sean's services witness the Holy Spirit's supernatural release to meet people with a heart of compassion and to touch their needs. In May of 2001, Sean received a Masters in Ministry from the Wagner Leadership Institute. Sean's writings have been published in several nation-wide publications. The Smith family currently resides in San Ramon, California.

Sean Smith Ministries—Pointblank International has been established with the purpose to **CARE:** **C**aptivate for Christ the hearts of a generation; **A**ctivate the army of God to fulfill its destiny; **R**each out to and reap lost souls; and **E**quip the body of Christ to meet the challenge of the Great Commission.

In the right hands, This Book will Change Lives!

Most of the people who need this message will not be looking for this book. To change their lives, you need to put a copy of this book in their hands.

> *But others (seeds) fell into good ground, and brought forth fruit, some a hundred-fold, some sixty-fold, some thirty-fold* (Matthew 13:8).

Our ministry is constantly seeking methods to find the good ground, the people who need this anointed message to change their lives. Will you help us reach these people?

> *Remember this—a farmer who plants only a few seeds will get a small crop. But the one who plants generously will get a generous crop* (2 Corinthians 9:6).

EXTEND THIS MINISTRY BY SOWING
3 BOOKS, 5 BOOKS, 10 BOOKS, OR MORE TODAY,
AND BECOME A LIFE CHANGER!

Thank you,

Don Nori Sr., Founder
Destiny Image
Since 1982

DESTINY IMAGE PUBLISHERS, INC.

"Speaking to the Purposes of God for This Generation
and for the Generations to Come."

VISIT OUR NEW SITE HOME AT
WWW.DESTINYIMAGE.COM

FREE SUBSCRIPTION TO DI NEWSLETTER

Receive free unpublished articles by top DI authors, exclusive

discounts, and free downloads from our best and newest books.

Visit www.destinyimage.com to subscribe.

Write to: Destiny Image
              P.O. Box 310
              Shippensburg, PA 17257-0310

Call: 1-800-722-6774

Email: orders@destinyimage.com

For a complete list of our titles or to place an order
online, visit www.destinyimage.com.